AF566843

365

QUESTIONS AND ANSWERS

Reprinted in 2015

An imprint of Om Books International

Corporate & Editorial Office
A 12, Sector 64, Noida 201 301
Uttar Pradesh, India
Phone: +91 120 477 4100
Email: editorial@ombooks.com
Website: www.ombooksinternational.com

Sales Office
107, Darya Ganj, New Delhi 110 002, India
Phone: +91 11 4000 9000, 2326 3363, 2326 5303
Fax: +91 11 2327 8091
Email: sales@ombooks.com
Website: www.ombooks.com

ISBN: 978-93-80070-79-7

Printed in India

10 9 8 7 6 5 4 3

365 QUESTIONS AND ANSWERS

An imprint of Om Books International

Contents

JANUARY

FEBRUARY

MARCH

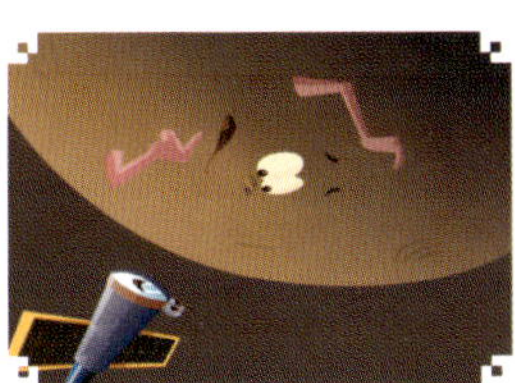

APRIL

MAY

JUNE

JULY

AUGUST

SEPTEMBER

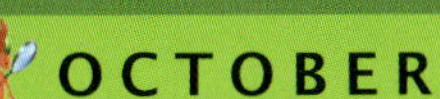

OCTOBER

NOVEMBER

DECEMBER

1. What is air?

Air is what we breathe. Air is what supports life on planet Earth. Air is what the plants need to grow. Air is all around us. In fact, air surrounds planet Earth like a blanket. Also known as the Earth's atmosphere, air is made up of many gases like Oxygen, Carbon-dioxide, Nitrogen, trace elements like Chlorine, Sulphur and Fluorine. It also has traces of water in the form of water vapour.

2. Can we see air?

We cannot see air as it is made up of colourless gases. In fact, Nitrogen, a colourless gas, makes for 78 per cent of air that we breathe. Hence, no colour is reflected and we cannot see air with the naked eye. We can, however, experience the presence of air around us in the movement of objects like trees, clothes and flags, which move or bend in the direction of winds and breezes.

3. Is there air in outer space?

The density of gases composing Earth's air blanket or atmosphere decreases with increasing altitude. Hence, as we move hundreds of kilometres above ground level towards outer space, air diminishes. The question whether the outer space is a vacuum is still unsolved. There is no air in space but a low density of gases like Hydrogen and Helium.

4. Why do balloons float?

Balloons are filled with a gas called Helium, which makes them lighter than the surrounding air. When balloons are set free in the air, they replace the heavier volume of surrounding air. This air is pulled down by gravity and as an equal reaction the balloon rises in the air. In a similar manner, balloons float in water as they are lighter and do not sink. It is a fascinating fact that although Hydrogen is the lightest gas, balloons are not filled with it because it is a highly flammable gas, that is, it can catch fire easily.

5. How is wind generated?

Some parts of the Earth receive direct rays from the Sun throughout the year and the air is always warm. Other places receive less sunlight, so the air is cooler. Wind is generated when air comes into motion. Warm air weighs less than cold air and thus rises above. Then, cool air moves in and replaces the rising warm air. This movement of air results in winds.

6. Why does water dry out in puddles?

When the Sun shines, the water in the puddles changes its physical form from liquid to gas. This process is called evaporation. Hence, we say that water evaporates from the puddles, and changes to water vapour that mixes with the air. This is the same principle that also works when we dry our wet clothes in the Sun.

7. What is steam?

We all know that water exists in three different forms—solid, liquid and gaseous. When water in liquid form is heated till its boiling point, it changes its form from liquid to gas. This is also known as steam. Like water, steam is colourless. You will be fascinated to know that steam can change its form back into liquid on being cooled. This process is called condensation.

8. How is ice formed?

When water is exposed to very cold temperature, it changes its form from liquid to solid. This is known as ice. The cold temperature at which water becomes ice is called the freezing point of water.

9. Why do soap bars sink in water?

Have you had a chance to see a bar of soap sink in a bucket of water? It happens because soap is able to break away the surface tension wall that is created by the water molecules. The water molecules bond together and create a wall on the surface. The soap molecules are bigger in size and thus able to break through those bonds and so the soap sinks.

10. What happens to sugar when mixed in a hot drink?

Sugar is composed of many molecules that are tightly packed with each other. A drink also has molecules but these are not as tightly packed. They keep moving around. When we add sugar to a hot drink, the moving water molecules hit against the sugar molecules. The sugar molecules then get separated from each other. After a while, we cannot see the sugar particles for they have completely dissolved in the drink. This process is faster in hot drinks than cold ones because the water molecules move around faster in hot drinks, breaking the sugar molecules faster. So, the next time you want to prepare lemonade, mix sugar in relatively warm water!

11. Why do fizzy drinks have bubbles?

In order to add fizz or froth to drinks, a gas called Carbon-dioxide is mixed into the drink. While mixing this gas, high pressure is built in the drink can as the gas gets trapped in the closed space. When the drink can is opened, the trapped gas molecules escape, creating bubbles.

12. Why can't we see in the dark?

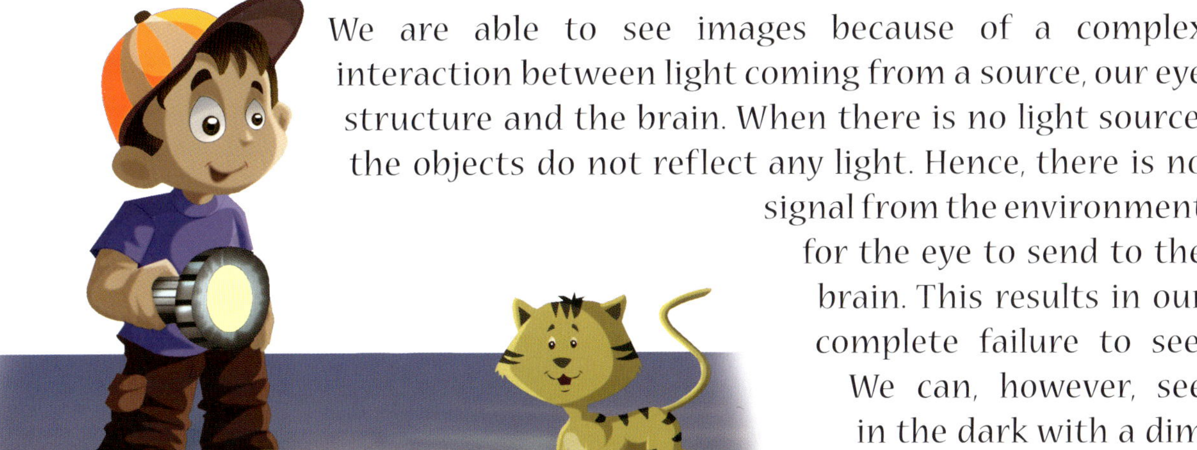

We are able to see images because of a complex interaction between light coming from a source, our eye structure and the brain. When there is no light source, the objects do not reflect any light. Hence, there is no signal from the environment for the eye to send to the brain. This results in our complete failure to see. We can, however, see in the dark with a dim source of light. But, in such cases, our colour perception is affected, and we see things in black and white.

13. How can we see our image in the mirror?

Mirrors have surfaces that are extremely smooth and polished. When light falls on such surfaces, it bounces back or reflects completely. So, when we stand in front of a mirror, the light reflected by us bounces back from the mirror surface, and we see our clear image.

14. Is light white in colour?

White is not the fundamental colour of light but is a spectrum of many colours. This was aptly demonstrated by the great scientist Newton. He passed white light through a prism and observed that the white beam of light split into a band of many colours.

15. How does a rainbow form?

A marvel of nature, the rainbow is an arc of light composed of a spectrum of colours, such as, red, orange, yellow, green, blue, indigo and violet. These colours make up the Sun's white light. A rainbow is seen when the Sun shines after the rain. When sunlight passes through a raindrop, it bends and scatters into its band of colours. These colours are then reflected from the back of the raindrop. These colours bend again as they pass through the front of the rain drop, and hence the curved rainbow is formed.

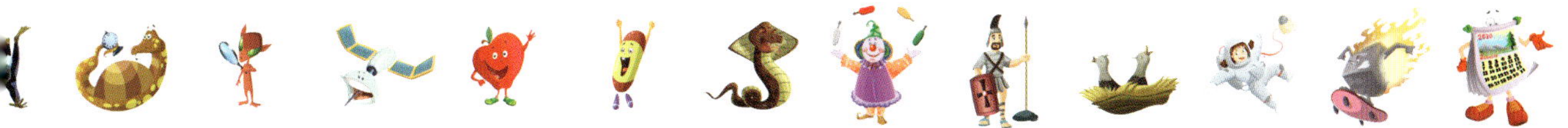

16. Why do we need to cover our windows with curtains on a hot, summer day?

As the Sun shines brightly outside, it radiates a lot of light and heat that enters our homes though the glass windows. When we drape our windows with curtains, the light and heat get reflected and the room remains cooler. By doing this, we can cut down on air-conditioning bills!

17. How do we see shadows?

Any object that blocks the straight path of light from a source will result in a shadow. This means if you stand in front of a light source, you block the path of light. The light then passes through the edges of your body and creates an outline that we call shadow.

18. What does opaque material mean?

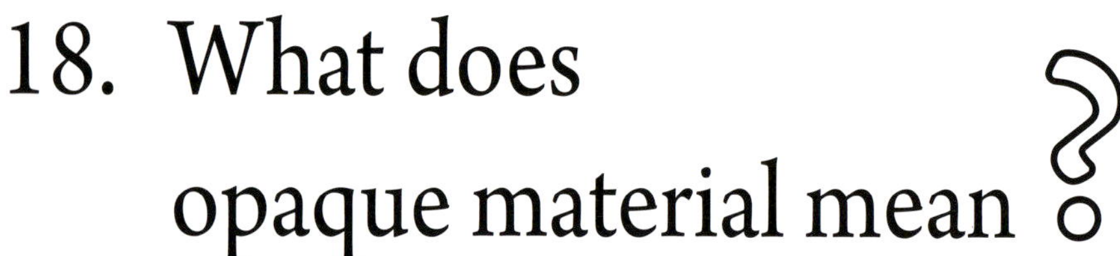

Light can pass through some materials, and is blocked by other materials. When the curtains are very thick, light does not pass through them. Such materials are called opaque materials. Sometimes, light can pass a little through some materials, also known as translucent materials. When any material allows light to pass through it completely, it's called a transparent material.

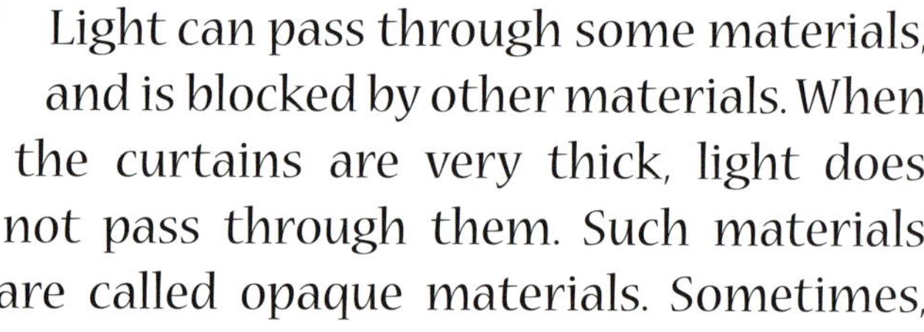

19. Can we see electricity?

We cannot see electricity, but we see its impact on our lives. There is nothing mysterious about why we cannot see electricity. It is made up of extremely tiny particles known as electrons. Electrons are invisible and consequently, so is electricity!

20. Where does electricity come from?

Electricity does not have any specialised source of origin. It results when a form of energy changes into electric current. The energy can be harnessed from water, steam, wind, Sun and chemical batteries. This transformation can be done through various sources, such as, power stations, wind turbines, water turbines and solar plants.

21. What is the meaning of soundproof?

A room or another such enclosed space is said to be soundproof when there is no physical contact in the airspace of the listener and in the airspace of the source of sound. For sound to be produced, there must be a vibration, and the object and the listener should both be in contact with air. The air contact should remain continuous without any vacuum. When this physical air contact is cut off, a soundproof environment is the result.

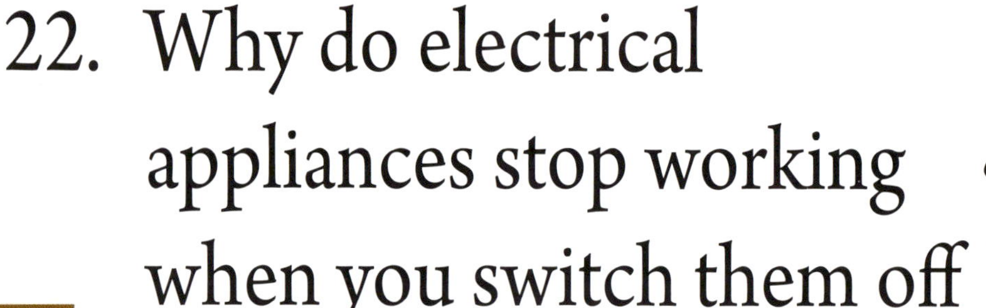

22. Why do electrical appliances stop working when you switch them off?

Appliances such as television, hair dryers, air conditioners and many others run on electricity. The electric current passes through a circuit and reaches the appliances through a wire. The switch at the end of the wire controls the flow of electric current. When we put the switch in an 'off' mode, electric current stops. Hence, the appliances stop working.

23. What instrument is used to measure electric current?

An ammeter is the instrument used to measure the electric current. Electric currents are measured in amperes (A), hence the name. Instruments used to measure smaller currents are called milliammeters or microammeters.

In earlier times, ammeters were rather bulky instruments and used in laboratories only. They relied on the magnetic field of the Earth for operation. By the late 19th century, improved versions of the ammeter were designed. They could be mounted in any position and allowed accurate measurements in electric power systems.

24. How does electricity reach our home?

The electricity that we enjoy at home is produced in huge power plants. These plants burn different kinds of fuel, such as, coal, natural gas or oil. When a fuel is burned, heat energy is released. This heat energy is then put through many processes in several stages. Eventually, a generator converts the energy into electricity. This electricity is then made to travel through transformers, which increase its voltage, so that it can easily travel through the distribution lines. After this is done, electricity reaches our homes, where we use it for heating and lighting purposes.

25. How can we see sound?

Sound waves are not visible to the naked eye. Sound is transferred by vibration, which occurs in the air that is already around us. These vibrations disturb the molecules already present in the air. This disturbance reaches us in the form of sound. Sound is only expansion and contraction in air! One can, though, see a sound graph on a music player.

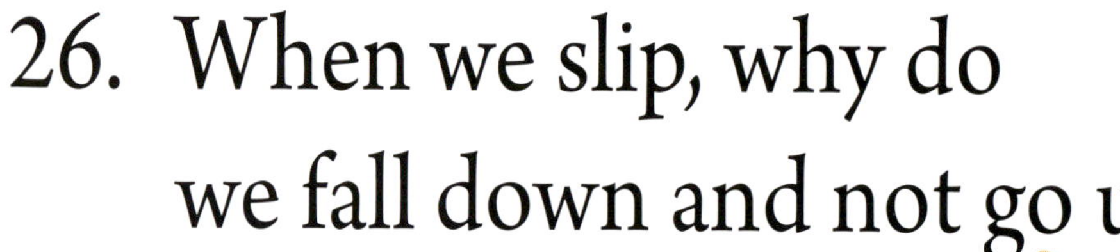

26. When we slip, why do we fall down and not go up?

It would be an unusual sight to see things going up rather than down when dropped or left suspended! But it is because of the Earth's gravity, a force that pulls things towards its centre that we all fall down when we slip.

27. How do magnets push and pull?

Magnets are very interesting as they can pull certain substances, such as, iron and nickel towards them without touching. Pull and Push are two forces that magnets exert when placed opposite to each other. Every magnet has two poles or ends, North and South. If we keep the two similar ends or poles of two magnets across each other, these will push each other away. If we keep the two opposite ends or poles across each other, the magnets will pull or attract each other.

28. How do magnets help explorers?

Magnets have been adapted in the form of a magnetised needle or compass that guides navigators and explorers to find their way when they travel. Our planet Earth has her own magnetised field, with two poles - North and South. When we look at the magnetic compass, the Earth's magnetic field causes the magnetised needle to automatically swing in the direction North-South. The next time you are out for an adventure, don't forget to carry a magnetic compass along with a route map to find your way!

29. Why are slides slippery?

While sliding, our bodies constantly rub against the slide surface. If the surface is rough, sliding will not be smooth because the resistance or friction will be more. Hence, slides are made slippery to reduce the friction or resistance. Material, such as, metal, if used for slides, will offer less resistance than cement or rough plastic.

30. How do brakes bring a bicycle to a halt?

While riding a bicycle, there is a lot of kinetic energy produced in the movement. In order to stop the bicycle, this moving energy needs to be reduced. This is done with the help of brakes. On pressing the brake padels, friction is created by the rubbing of the rubber clamps attached to the wheels. This slows down the kinetic energy and the bicycle stops.

31. What makes objects heavy?

Every object is pulled down by Earth's gravitational force. The more the mass of an object, the greater is the gravitational force that pulls it down. Hence, objects become heavy to lift.

1. When was the first farming done?

According to research done by archaeologists, modern man has lived for almost 200,000 years. Yet, till about 13,000 years ago, he was dependent only on hunting animals and gathering wild fruits for his food. Farming, as an activity, did not emerge at one single place. But it emerged as a way of life across the globe, beginning with South-East Asia. It also emerged independently in other areas of Africa, Mexico, South America and eastern USA.

2. Who is Lucy?

Lucy is the best-known female specimen of the species *Australopithecus afarensis*, the human ancestors believed to have walked Earth 3.2 million years ago. The fossils, discovered at Hadar in Ethiopia in 1974, have helped to draw conclusions that *Australopithecus afarensis* could walk like humans, and did not just depend on climbing trees.

3. Why is the Stone Age so called?

The Stone Age is so named for it was during this period (some 2.6 million years ago) that man made tools for the first time, and he used stone to carve out useful tools. With these intelligent tools, it became very easy for man to hunt.

4. What kind of tools and weapons were used in the prehistoric times?

Our ancestors started making tools and weapons about 2.6 million years ago. The first tools were made from stone. In the beginning, stones were not chiselled, and were used in their pre-existing shapes and forms. With time, man started making stone tools by removing flakes and blades from a stone. Bones, horns and tusks were also used. The bow and arrow, and the spear were important inventions. Stone tools were replaced by bronze and iron tools, which were sturdier than the stone tools.

5. How was the first fire lit?

The story behind how the first fire was lit is not a very conclusive one. It is believed that perhaps the first fire was lit from a stream of lava or a burning tree trunk set on fire by lightening.

6. Why was fire useful?

The discovery of fire played a vital role in the evolution of man as a social and cultural being. Initially, man used fire for warming up, cooking and protection from wild animals. Over the course of time, he must have accidentally baked clay and mud in fire and discovered the art of pottery. With time, metals were smelted and utensils and advanced tools were made with the help of fire.

7. How did people in the Stone Age light fire?

It is believed that man in the Stone Age discovered fire by rubbing two stones against each other. This would create friction and sparks would fly off. He would ignite dry grass with these sparks and start a fire.

8. What kind of art existed in prehistoric times?

The early man depicted his ideas and beliefs with the help of visual images. The images were mostly geometric in shape. The depictions also included animal figures and mixed animal-human figures. Man decorated the cave he lived in with his art work, where scenes like hunting were etched. Later, decorating pottery and making clay jewellery took the prehistoric art to a higher level.

9. What kind of clothes did people of prehistoric times wear?

Archaeologists believe that the earlier forms of clothing included drapes made from leaves, animal skin, fur and grass. The aspect of covering bodies mainly resulted from harsh weather conditions. As the wave of civilised society grew, clothing took on a more social meaning.

10. When was the first town built?

With farming emerging as a way of producing food, people started coming together in sharing a common place for living. The earliest settlements are considered to be the one at Jericho, around 9,000 years ago, which is in the present-day Israeli-occupied West Bank. The second was at Catal Huyuk in southern Turkey.

11. Who were Adam and Eve?

According to the Bible, Adam was the first man on Earth. He was created by God out of the dust. Eve is considered to be the first woman and was created by God as a companion for Adam.

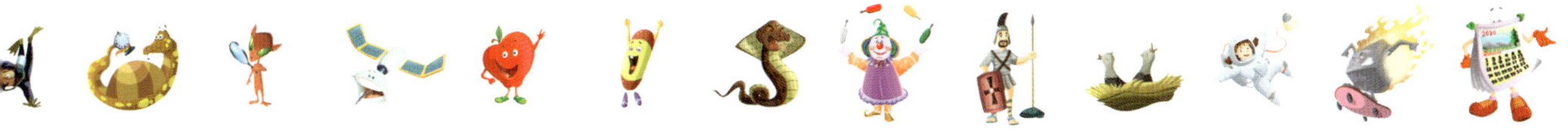

12. Which is the world's oldest city?

A city is different from a town or village primarily because it has specialised labour groups settling down in a common place. Tell Hamoukar in north-eastern Syria is the world's oldest city. Earlier Sumer was considered to be the oldest city, until excavations done at Tell Hamoukar revealed the presence of a city that existed in mid-fourth millennium BC.

13. Which were the first-grown crops?

It is believed that wheat and barley have been grown for 10,000 years. They were the first wild plants to be noticed by the Stone Age man, who collected them to make food.

14. Where did the first humans live?

Humans have descended from the Hominidae (or Great Ape family). The species from which modern man is thought to have evolved is the *Homo Habilis* that lived more than 2.5 million years ago and *Homo Erectus* that lived more than 1.25 million years ago. These have originated from earlier hominids (the *Australopithecus afarensis*, *Australopithecus africanus*, to name a few). Most of the partial skeletal remains have been found in East Africa (Ethiopia and Kenya) and South East Asia. The most famous hominid is 'Lucy' found at Hadar, Ethiopia in 1974. So, around 200,000 years ago and then 70,000 years ago, modern *Homo Sapiens* established themselves. So far, Africa appears to have been the cradle for early human development. Laetoli close to Olduvia Gorge (Tanzania), Hadar (Ethiopia), Sterkfontein Caves (Johannesburg, South Africa) are some of the sites where Hominid remains have been discovered.

15. When did life on Earth begin?

Numerous studies conducted by various scientists conclude that Earth was formed 4.5 billion years ago. After the surface of the Earth was cooled, plants and animals began to appear. A study of the evolution of plants and animals highlights that they first appeared 550 million years ago. First came the marine invertebrates (the shell-making ammonites) followed by fish, amphibians, reptiles, birds, mammals and finally human beings. A group of scientists, who study rocks at the Akilia Island, suggest that living organism have inhabited Earth since 3.85 billion years ago. They base their theory on the microfossils of animals, plants and other bacteria five-thousandth of a millimetre in length that they found in the rocks of Western Australia's Marble Bar.

16. How do we know about pre-historic life?

Scientists learn about pre-historic life by studying remains of plants, animals and other objects, their fossil imprints, old rocks and human bones. From plant and animal fossils, scientists can conclude that the area at that time was either wet and warm or dry and warm. Through their study on human evolution, scientists believe that 7 million years ago, the African Apes evolved into three distinct species. One species was of humans and the other two were gorillas and chimpanzees. After humans evolved, they left information in the form of drawings and inscription on cave walls. We can learn of how the ancient man lived by studying these inscriptions.

17. How did man live in the Stone Age?

The Stone Age existed for 2 million years. Early Man was larger and taller than the man of today and even had a larger brain. He lived in caves and under cliffs and roamed from one place to another in search of food and shelter. The Stone Age man survived on fruits, plants, roots and other wild plants. Then, he slowly learnt to hunt animals and discovered fire. For protection, the Stone Age men formed a group and stayed in camps. Scientists have found evidence of such camps.

18. Who built the pyramids?

A pyramid is a huge stone or brick structure that stands on a square base with four sloping sides meeting at a height. In world history, pyramids have been built in various parts at different times. However, the most famous pyramids are those of ancient Egypt, built by the Egyptian kings. The first pyramids were ordered by the famous kings Khufu, his son Khafre and his grandson Menkure in the 26th century BC. The first of these, the Great Pyramid, is the largest ever built. Pyramids were also built in pre-Columbian civilisations in Central and South America. Some pyramids exist in Sudan, Southwest Asia and Greece, too.

19. Why did pharaohs need pyramids?

Pharaohs were Egyptian kings. They wanted the construction of pyramids as places where they would be buried. The kings feared that their dead remains would be disturbed by grave robbers. Hence, they desired an enclosed space. You will be amazed to know that the valuables stored with the dead bodies of kings were stolen by robbers on many occasions.

20. What is mummification?

The process of mummification is unique to the earliest and ancient Egyptian civilisation. In this process, the dead bodies were preserved by applying a balm and wrapping the whole body with linen. The mummified bodies were then kept in coffins and buried.

21. How were the bodies mummified?

The process of mummification was carried out in two stages: embalming of the dead body and covering the embalmed body with linen. In the first stage, the bodies were rubbed with palm oil and Nile water and the internal organs were cleaned out. This was done because the organs are the first to decompose. The heart was however kept intact. The internal organs and the body were then dried for 40 days. After rubbing with oils, the bodies were then wrapped with linen, amidst chanting by priests to ward off evil spirits.

22. Who was Tutankhamun?

Pharaoh Tutankhamun is one of the most famous Egyptian kings. Though his rule lasted for a very short time of nine years, his mysterious death at the age of 19 made him a subject of study and speculation. After studying his 3300-years old DNA samples taken from his mummified body, geneticists have tried to reconstruct the events leading to his death. The scientists say that Tutankhamun died because of a malarial attack, following a leg fracture.

23. What were the Seven Wonders of the Ancient World?

The list of Seven Wonders of Ancient World was a compilation done in the medieval times by some Greek authors to bring out the seven great structures of the world, man-made or natural. Though the list is constantly revised, the original list consisted of some breathtaking marvels like the Great Pyramid of Giza, the Hanging Gardens of Babylon, the Statue of Zeus at Olympia, the Temple of Artemis at Ephesus, the Mausoleum of Maussollos at Halicarnassus, the Colossus of Rhodes and the Lighthouse of Alexandria.

24. Who are some of the famous ancient Greeks?

Greece has been the home of many famous personalities, including rulers, philosophers, scientists, mathematicians, poets and sculptors. Alexander the Great is considered to be one of greatest military rulers. Philosophers like Aristotle, Plato and Socrates contributed valuable lessons on life, ethics and education to the world. Archimedes, an astronomer, added value in the field of Mathematics and Science. The epic poems, Iliad and Odyssey by Homer are irreplaceable in world literature. Greece surely has given the world a lot of geniuses!

25. When were the Olympics first held?

Greeks were the first to have invented a series of athletic contests in honour of their gods. The first Olympics were held in Greece in early 700 BC and were held every four years. An ivory and gold statue of God Zeus, also one of the seven ancient wonders, was built to commemorate the first games. The first modern Olympics were held in Athens in 1896. The winners of these games were crowned with a wreath made of olive tree branches.

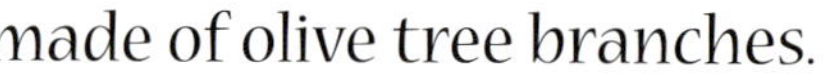

26. When was swimming introduced in Olympic Games?

Although swimming did not find a place in the ancient Games, it was introduced in the Athens Olympics of 1896. Four swimming contests were held, but only for men. Women were first allowed to swim in the Stockholm Olympic Games in 1912.

27. What is fascinating about Greek mythology?

Greek mythology is embedded in religion and comprises of myths and legends about gods, heroes, the culture and nature of the world. The main source of understanding Greek mythology is found in the literature from that region; the most famous works being of Homer. The largest single theme in Greek mythology is the battle of Troy.

28. Who was Alexander the Great?

Alexander emerged as a powerful Greek leader and soldier at a young age of 20. He was determined to conquer the world. This quest led him through some of the most important ancient cities and civilisations, like the ones in Syria, Egypt and Indus Valley. He ended up conquering much of what was considered to be civilised at that time!

29. Who built the Great Wall of China?

This great structure in China is a series of stone and earthen walls built between the periods 5th century BC and 16th century. The main aim was to defend the northern borders of the Chinese empire during the rule of its successive rulers. It is the world's longest man-made structure, measuring 6400 kilometres. There are, however, three walls that make up the Great Wall; each wall being constructed in a different dynasty.

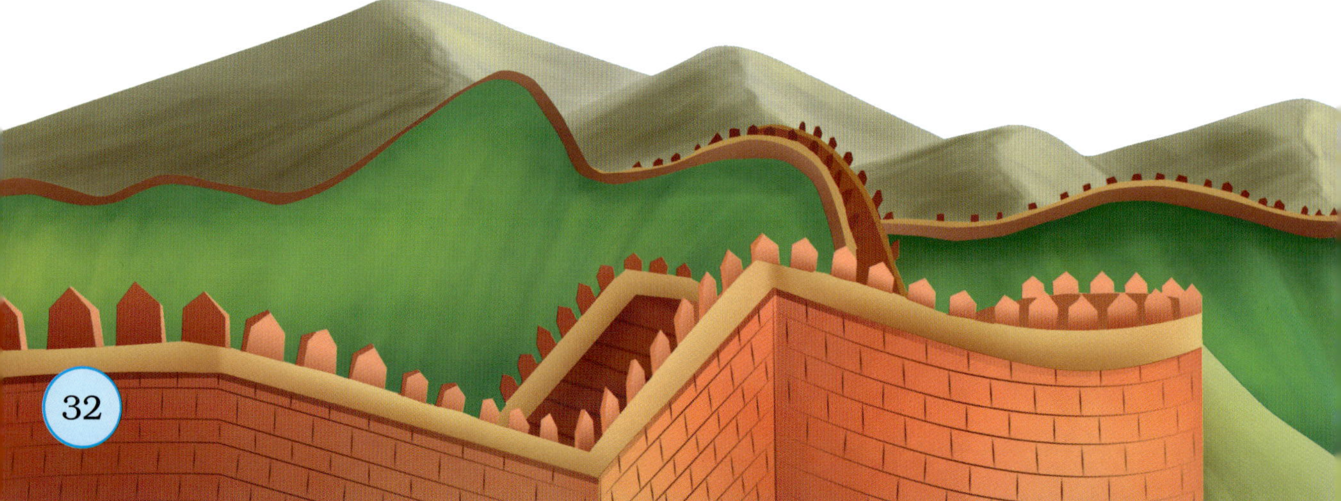

1. Which weapons did the Roman soldiers use?

In the ancient times, the Roman Army was controlled by the king to conquer other countries. The soldiers were trained well to fight and defend themselves. They fought with swords and daggers, and carried a long spear, which they threw at their enemies. They also carried a shield for protection and wore armour and helmet for extra safety.

2. What war tactics did the Roman soldiers follow?

The war tactics used by the Roman Army were rather organised. The soldiers always stood in lines, with adequate support standing behind. The front row would first throw javelins on the enemy and then they would fight with the swords. When the front row of soldiers was dead, the second row started to attack.

3. Where did dinosaurs come from?

Dinosaurs did not appear as we know them. They evolved from amphibians and reptiles over a period of millions of years. A group of reptiles called Archosaurs, living in the late Permian period, had mastered the skill of hunting on land. Around 200 million years ago, with the introduction of the Triassic Period, these reptiles further evolved into more sophisticated beings. Their body became more upright and they developed a skull and legs under their bodies. After these developments, they came to be called the dinosaurs.

4. Which were the largest animals that ever flew in the skies?

Pterosaurs were the largest animals to fly in the skies. Pterosaurs were reptiles that lived 140 million years ago with the dinosaurs from the Triassic to the Cretaceous period. They were fierce animals and are also called the 'Winged Lizards'. A Chinese Pterosaur had a 5 feet wingspan and Quetzalcoatlus, which is the largest Pterosaur, had a wingspan of 36 feet. The smallest Pterosaur, Anurognathus, was only as big as a sparrow. They had very keen eyesight, sharp claws to lift their prey and pointed teeth to tear it apart.

5. Describe the first fish?

The fish was the first vertebrate to inhabit the Earth and from it came all the land animals – the mammoths, dinosaurs and large cats like tigers. The first fish evolved to become jawless fish. The jawless fish did not have a lower jaw and therefore could not eat large preys. Astraspis and Arandaspis were the most popular jawless fish. They were six inches long and had a hole on their head through which they sucked food. These fish looked like tadpoles and usually hunted in shallow waters and slowly began to move to land to look for more food. The jawless fish existed 490 to 410 million years ago.

6. What do you know about crocodiles?

Crocodiles have lived on Earth since even before the dinosaurs but they looked different from the crocodiles of today. All species of past and present that belong to the family of *Crocodylidae* are called crocodiles. Alligators, Ghariyals and Caimans, too, are included in the crocodile family.

7. Did the early mammals lay eggs?

We all know that mammals do not lay eggs; they give birth to young ones. However, scientists believe that just like the semi-aquatic platypus, mammals in early periods laid eggs, in particular the Spiny Anteater *(Echidna)* and the duck-billed platypus. Both these animals come from Australia. Although the two creatures have mammary glands they do not give birth to babies, rather produce eggs. After observing and understanding these animals, scientists have suggested that early mammals, too, reproduced by laying eggs.

8. Which was the biggest ever land animal?

As you might have guessed, the biggest ever land animal was a dinosaur. It belonged to the Sauropod family. Scientists have named it *Amphicoelias fragillimus*. We know that it was the largest land animal because a fossil of this dinosaur's remains was discovered by scientists. Now, this fossil was not complete. The broken bit found by scientists was 1.5 metres long. It is believed that the entire fossil would have been 2.7 metres long, giving this dinosaur immense height.

9. How big were the biggest dinosaurs?

The biggest dinosaurs were known as the Sauropods. They were huge, but had tiny heads. Because of their great size and weight, they moved very slowly. Also, contrary to what we expect from large dinosaurs, the Sauropods were not ferocious dinosaurs — they were herbivorous and ate plants! They had very long necks and a huge tail. This balanced the two ends of their bodies.

10. How small were the smallest dinosaurs?

The smallest dinosaur, *Compsognathus*, was about 60 centimetres long. It weighed approximately the same as a chicken. Later, Microraptor who was of a crow's size was found in China. It was 40 centimetres long.

11. Where did the dinosaurs live?

According to the palaeontologists, the dinosaurs lived on all the continents. However, it is very difficult to clearly mention the habitats of dinosaurs as very little fossil data is available. At times, a few plants and animals are found which existed in the times of dinosaurs but still nothing much can be said about their environment.

12. How were fossils made?

Fossils are formed through various processes of the nature. In arid areas of the world, fossils of animals and humans were formed because the arid climate completely dried their dead bodies. This preserved the bodies for thousands of years and provided us with their fossils. Fossils can also be formed by freezing. If a dead body is continuously frozen for thousands of years, this also forms a fossil. Scientists have discovered the remains of many animals from the Ice Age through this process of fossilisation. Another process through which fossils are formed is called carbonisation. In this process, the dead body of the creature leaves its impression in the form of carbon, upon rocks or trees.

13. What did dinosaurs eat?

Most of the dinosaurs were herbivores (plant eaters) but some of them were carnivores (meat eaters). It is very important in any food chain that there are more organisms at the lower levels of the chain. This is because if the transfer of the food energy is inadequate, then much of the energy is wasted. During the age of dinosaurs (Mesozoic Era), the variety of plants was much greater in number than the animals.

14. How fast could dinosaurs run?

The smallest dinosaurs could run as fast as a racehorse (64 kilometres per hour). The highest running speed of the dinosaurs could differ from 37 kilometres per hour to 88 kilometres per hour. The highest figure (88.6 km per hour) is similar to the speed of fastest land animals in today's age like the North American Pronghorn.

15. What happened to the dinosaurs?

Fossil evidences show that the number and variety of dinosaurs declined in the last 10 million years of the Cretaceous Period. During this time, the climate on Earth became much cooler and drier. Dinosaurs became extinct since they could not adapt themselves to the environmental changes, which happened due to various reasons. For example, around the same time, a large asteroid struck the Earth and a 240 kilometres crater was formed in the Yucatan Peninsula in Mexico. This could have caused extremely cold months or years because of the dust in the atmosphere. Likewise, many volcanic eruptions took place around that time. Huge quantities of lava, volcanic ash and poisonous gas led to a lot of climatic change, all leading to the extinction of dinosaurs.

16. Which was the first artificial satellite to be launched in space?

In October 1957, Soviet Union (now Russia) launched the first artificial satellite, Sputnik I, in space. It was roughly the size of a beach ball and took 98 minutes to orbit the Earth. Sputnik I was important for it inspired other nations, especially USA to develop their space programmes. It also helped in understanding the density of Earth's atmosphere.

17. Who was the first living being to be sent to space?

Laika, a dog, is recognised as the first living being to be sent to space. Laika, a three-year-old mutt was sent in Soviet Union's Sputnik II in November 1957. However, it turned out to be unfortunate as Laika could not make it back to Earth.

18. Which is the biggest rocket ever sent into space?

Saturn V (Saturn Five) is the largest and the most powerful rocket ever sent into space. At 364-feet high, this rocket was designed under the guidance of Wernher von Braun also known as the rocket man. Since the rocket was huge, National Aeronautics and Space Administration (NASA) had to build a new building, the Vertical Assembly Building. This is one of the largest buildings in the world. It is amazing that all of the 12 launches with Saturn V were successful.

19. What do rockets carry to space?

A rocket is a vehicle that carries the spacecraft which has astronauts, satellites and equipments to space. When a rocket is launched, the fuel packed under pressure is released from its body. This release gives a powerful push to the rocket, making it go upwards at high speed.

20. Is there a telescope in space?

A telescope called the Hubble Telescope (named after Edwin Hubble) was placed in space in April 1990. This telescope completes a spin around the Earth in 97 minutes. The Hubble Telescope captures thousands of pictures of Earth and galaxies in the Universe and sends it back to Earth.

21. Why does the Moon change its shape?

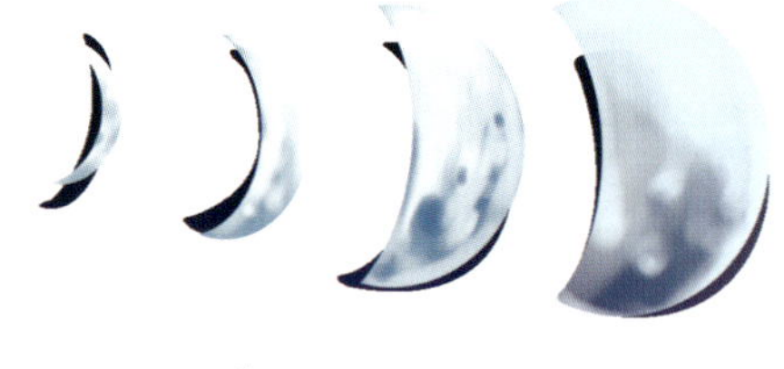

We all know that the Moon does not have its own light. We are able to see the Moon from the Earth's surface because half of its side is lit up by the Sun. The other half faces away from the Sun and so is dark. The Moon orbits around the Earth every 29 ½ days. As the Moon moves around the Earth, we see more and more of its lit side; hence the changing shapes of the Moon.

22. Which planet was found by accident?

Uranus was accidentally discovered by Sir William Herschel in 1791. Until 1690, many astronomers had noticed this planet but understood it to be a star. When Sir William Herschel was studying stars, he noticed that one "star" was different from the others and seemed much farther away from the Sun and the Earth. This "star" was then named Uranus.

23. How many moons does Uranus have?

Uranus has 27 moons. They come in a variety of forms. Some are rocky, icy, or a combination of both. The smallest moon, called Miranda, has a 16-kilometre high cliff. You will be amazed to know that Mount Everest, the highest mountain peak on Earth, is only about half as high. Arial is the most recently formed moon.

24. What keeps the planets moving around the Sun?

According to Isaac Newton, planets keep moving around in their orbits around the Sun. The force that pulls the planets in the direction of the Sun is a result of the mass of the Sun and the individual planets.

25. Who was the first woman to have walked in space?

Valentina Tereshkova was the first woman to have walked in space in 1963. A Russian cosmonaut, Tereshkova was launched in space in the spacecraft Vostok 6. The flight took 70.8 hours and made 48 orbits of Earth. When she returned from space, Tereshkova was honoured with the title 'Hero of the Soviet Union'. Later, she also received the United Nations Gold Medal of Peace.

26. What was the mission of Apollo II ?

In 1961, President of USA, John F. Kennedy dreamt of sending human beings to Moon. This dream was fulfilled in 1969, when the space shuttle Apollo 11 took off on July 16, 1969. Neil Armstrong, Edwin Aldrin and Michael Collins were the astronauts aboard Apollo 11. While Armstrong and Aldrin walked on the surface of the Moon, Collins stayed in the orbit and conducted experiments and clicked pictures. The astronauts placed a U.S. flag on the Moon. Since, Armstrong was the first to get off the space craft, his name is etched in history as the first person to step on the Moon.

27. Who first drove on the Moon ?

On July 31, 1971, Apollo 15 astronauts David Scott and James Irwin drove the Lunar Roving Vehicle or LRV on the surface of the Moon. It was the first automobile ride outside the Earth's atmosphere. The LRV was an amazing piece of technology, a two-seater with electric power. It was developed in just 17 months.

28. Why don't we float off into space?

Gravity is the attractive force that keeps us from flying off into space. Since our weight is greater than the weight of the air that we displace around us, we are held to the centre of the Earth.

29. What causes the lunar eclipse?

Lunar eclipse or eclipse of the Moon occurs on a full moon night. It occurs because the Earth blocks the Sun's light from reaching the Moon as the Moon passes behind the Earth.

30. What are asteroids?

Asteroids, also known as minor planets, are rocky and metallic objects that orbit around the Sun. However, these are not considered as planets for their small sizes. It is believed that asteroids are the left-over particles formed after massive collisions that occurred in space when the Solar System was being formed. Some asteroids are also found inside Earth's orbit.

31. Could an asteroid hit Earth?

Asteroids are found in Earth's orbit. Some also approach the Earth's atmosphere at great speeds. Asteroids that cross the Earth's path and are on their way to colliding with the Earth's surface are called meteoroids. However, on striking our atmosphere at great speed, part of the meteoroid is lit into a spark of light, while the non-burnt part could hit the Earth's surface.

1. What is an asteroid belt?

The asteroid belt is a region between the inner planets and outer planets where thousands of asteroids have been orbiting around the Sun. The asteroid belt between Mars and Jupiter is known as the main asteroid belt. Ceres has been considered to be the largest asteroid, taking about 25 per cent of the asteroid belt space.

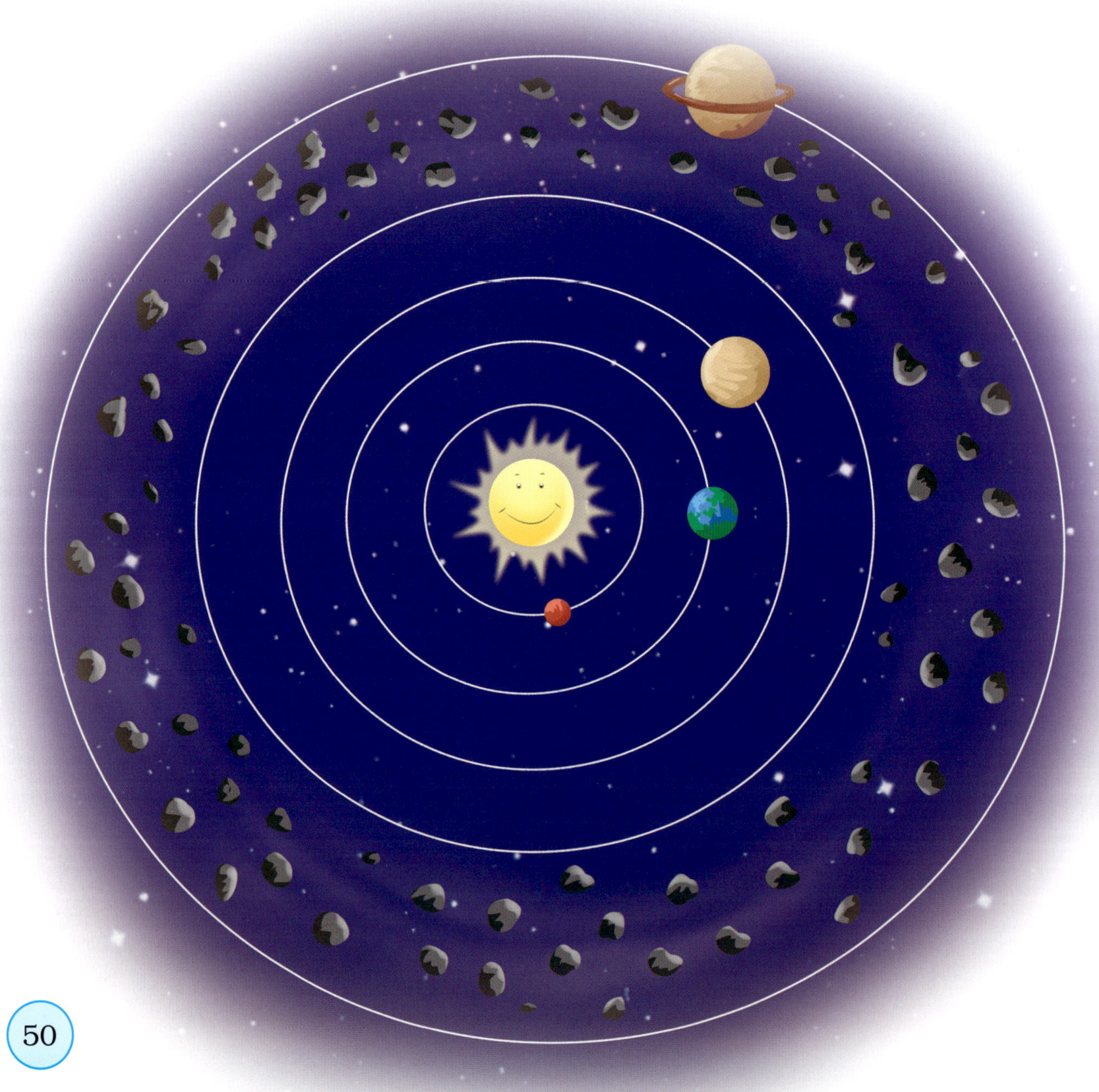

2. What causes a solar eclipse?

A solar eclipse or eclipse of the Sun occurs when the Moon passes between the Sun and the Earth. It then either covers the Sun partially or completely.

3. What is a light year?

We know that our Universe is huge and widespread. It is not possible to measure its distances in units like metres and kilometres. Hence, we use a special distance measuring unit in space. It is called the light year. Scientists have calculated that one light year is equal to 9,500,000,000,000 kilometres.

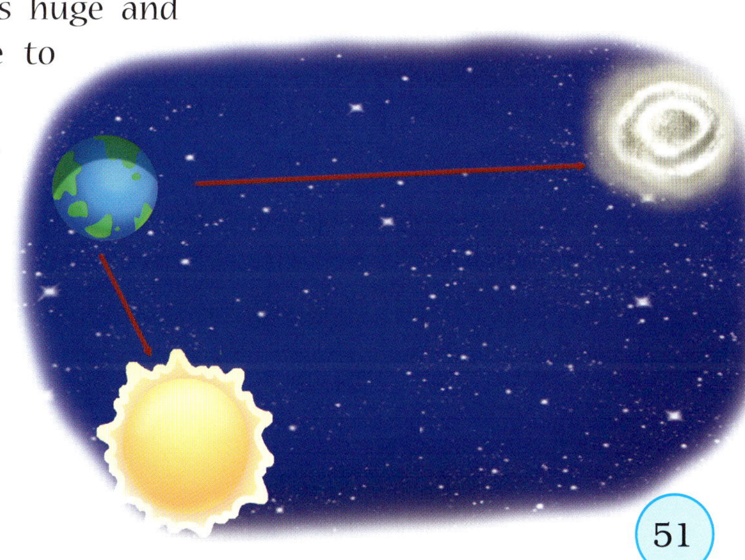

4. How big is the Solar System?

We live in a huge Solar System, where all the planets revolve, or orbit, around the Sun. It has been indeed difficult to find out exactly how large our Solar System is. However, scientists have calculated an approximate distance between our Earth and the Sun. The Sun is the star closest to our planet and it is 93 million miles away from us. That is why even though it is one million times larger than the size of our Earth, the Sun appears much smaller. So huge is our Solar System, that even if we travelled at the speed of light, it would take us one hundred thousand years to cross it!

5. How many planets are there in the Solar System?

Our Solar System is made up of eight planets. They are—Mercury, Venus, Earth, Mars, Jupiter, Saturn, Uranus and Neptune. Of these, Mercury is the closest to the Sun and Neptune is the farthest. Until very recently, there was also a ninth planet in our Solar System, called Pluto. However, it is a dwarf planet. Apart from Pluto, there are two other dwarf planets- Eris and Ceres. There are also hundreds of thousands of other minor planets, like asteroids.

6. How old are the planets?

Our Solar System is extremely old. It went through years and years of change before the human species existed. Scientists have estimated that our Earth is 4.6 billion years old. They believe that the other planets must also be at least as old as the Earth, although there is no solid evidence to validate this fact. We still live on a wise old planet, as 4.6 billion years has nine zeroes!

7. Which is the blue planet?

Our home, the Earth, is actually the blue planet! There are several reasons for this name. First, our Earth is mostly made up of water—almost 70 per cent of the entire planet is water! This is why, when a satellite takes a picture of the Earth, it looks mostly blue in colour. Another reason why our planet is called the blue planet is because our atmosphere—the sky—is also blue in colour.

8. Is the Moon flying off into space?

As strange and unlikely as it sounds, the Moon really is flying off into space. Like our Earth, the Sun also holds gravitational force. The Sun's gravity pulls the Moon towards itself, little by little. The result is that the Moon is moving further away from us by 1.5 centimetres every year. Millions of years ago, the Moon appeared ten times bigger than it does now, because it used to be a lot closer then!

9. How big is the Sun?

Remember how huge our Solar System is? The Sun is so huge that it alone makes up for 99 per cent of the Solar System's mass. Its size is so immense that 11,900 Earths could fit into it. It is also extremely heavy and massive. It weighs as much as 333,000 Earths!

10. What is the Sun made up of?

Does it look like the Sun is made up of heat and fire? Well, it is actually almost entirely made up of two gases called hydrogen and helium. These gases are the lightest elements you could find in the Universe. For every one million atoms of hydrogen in the Sun, there are 98,000 atoms of helium, 850 of oxygen, 360 of carbon, 120 of neon, 110 of nitrogen, 40 of magnesium, 35 of iron and 35 of silicon. So, even though the Sun is mostly made up of hydrogen, this gas only makes up 72 per cent of the Sun's mass. Helium constitutes 26 per cent of its mass. The remaining 2 per cent of the mass is made up of the other elements.

11. How hot is the Sun?

We all realise that the Sun is extremely hot. The temperature of its outermost surface is about 10,000 Fahrenheit, which is equal to 5,600 degrees Celsius. As we go deeper into the Sun's layers, the temperature increases. Its core is 27,000,000 Fahrenheit (15,000,000 degrees Celsius). The temperature also rises as we move from the Sun's surface upwards, into the solar atmosphere. But we are so far away from the Sun that we are luckily not burnt by its rays!

12. Where does the Sun go at night?

The Sun, in fact, does not move at all, but stays where it is. It is our Earth that moves. We all know that the Earth is round in shape. It rotates about a tilted axis and takes almost 24 hours to complete one rotation. This is also the reason that one day is made up of 24 hours. So, only half of the Earth faces the Sun at one time. The other half faces away from it and is therefore dark. This is the half where it is night on Earth. Next time you tuck into bed at night, remember that your friends in distant countries are enjoying a sunny afternoon!

13. How does the Moon shine?

Technically, the Moon does not shine by itself, because it has no light of its own. It appears to shine because of the Sun's light that reaches it. However, the Moon does not shine as brightly as the Sun, because its surface absorbs most of the light that falls on it from the Sun. It reflects only 7 per cent of the Sun's light and therefore, glows softly.

14. Is there a man on Moon?

When you look at the Moon at night, does a face-like structure smile back at you from it? The truth is there is no man on the Moon. The face that we see is only because the Moon's surface is rough. Thus, it appears dark at certain spots and lighter at others, which gives it a face-like appearance. We send space mission on the Moon, sometimes. Neil Armstrong was the first human to land on the Moon. However, there are no people living there!

15. Which planet has the biggest moon?

Jupiter is the planet with the biggest Moon. Jupiter's Moon is called Ganymede. It has a diameter of 3,280 miles. This Moon is even larger than the planet Mercury and the dwarf planet, Pluto!

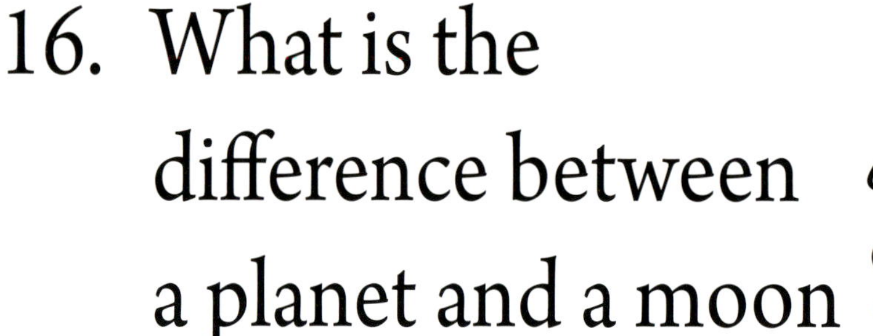

16. What is the difference between a planet and a moon?

There is only one essential difference that separates a planet from a moon. A planet orbits around a star, while a moon orbits around a planet. For example, our Earth orbits around the sun, which is a star. Therefore, the Earth is a planet and our moon orbits around the Earth.

17. Are there snowballs in space?

Technically speaking, there are snowballs in space! A number of comets are made up of ice. There is also dust and rocks in them, but the comets are mostly made up of ice. So, these comets are like giant snowballs zooming around in space.

18. What are shooting stars?

Have you ever made a wish on a shooting star? It is beautiful shiny object in space that you spot in the sky once in a while. These shiny objects are known as meteors to scientists. Meteors are actually big chunks of rock that fly through the space at great speeds. Because of the immense speed, these large lumps of rock begin to heat up and eventually catch fire. The fire makes them glow. This is what you see as a shooting star!

19. Which planet orbits the Sun the fastest?

The planet Mercury is the closest to the Sun. Thus, it has to revolve around a much smaller circle to complete one revolution about the Sun. Because of the small distance, it takes only 88 days to orbit the Sun once, while our Earth takes 365 days to complete one revolution, because it is much further away from the Sun!

20. Which is the hottest planet?

Venus is the hottest planet in our Solar System. It is second-closest to the Sun. The temperature on its surface is almost an average of 464 degrees Celsius. It is so hot because of its extremely dense atmosphere, upon which clouds of carbon dioxide and sulphuric acid float. The carbon dioxide on Venus traps heat in its atmosphere and does not let it escape back into the space. It is because of this heat that strong winds blow on Venus, with a speed of 300 kilometres per hour!

21. Which planet has rings?

As many as four planets have rings in our Solar System. They are—Jupiter with three rings, Saturn and Uranus both with thirteen rings each and Neptune with five rings. These rings are masses of gas that have formed about these planets.

22. How many stars are there?

In the Universe, stars cluster together to form galaxies. With the help of powerful telescopes, scientists have discovered that there are billions of galaxies in the Universe and each galaxy holds billions of stars. Our own galaxy, the Milky Way, holds about two hundred billion stars alone!

23. What is a galaxy?

A galaxy is essentially a huge mass of stars, dust and gases. It is disc-like in shape. The group of stars, dust and gas is held together in this disc-like manner because of gravitational force. It can take one a few thousand or several hundreds of light years to cross a galaxy!

24. Why is our galaxy called the Milky Way?

The Milky Way is the galaxy that we live in. From space, it looks like a thick, glowing band of stars clustered tightly together. This looks like a flat, white path. Hence, our galaxy is named the Milky Way. If you were to travel from one end of our galaxy to another, it would take you 100,000 light years to do so! And if you wanted to cross the galaxy vertically, in thickness, that would take you 10,000 light years.

25. Are all galaxies the same?

No, not all galaxies are the same. They exist in numerous sizes and shapes. Sometimes they stand alone and sometimes in pairs. Sometimes galaxies are even grouped together to form a huge cluster. Our own galaxy, the Milky Way, is spiral in shape and contains two hundred billion stars.

26. What is the Red Giant?

Red Giants are basically stars. As the name suggests, they are extremely huge—they may be ten times, or even hundreds of times larger than the Sun. Red Giants are comparatively lighter than other bodies in the space. The atmosphere of Red Giant stars is inflated or puffed up and the temperature at its surface is much lower than that of other stars. This gives it a red glow. Hence, it is given the name the Red Giant.

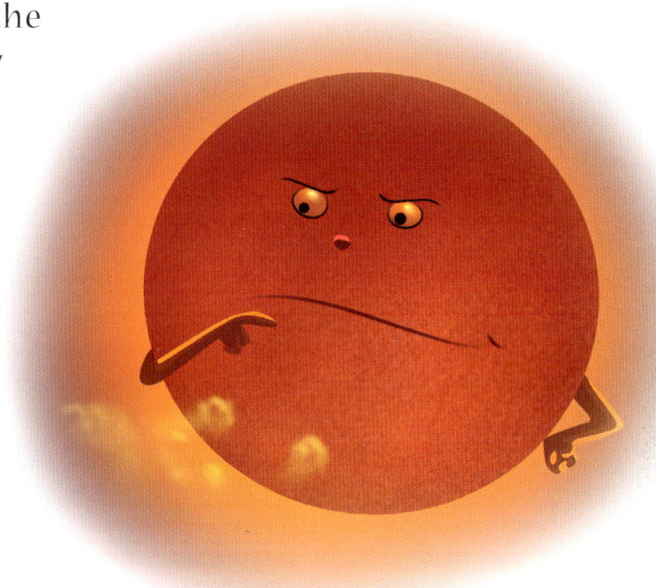

27. What are constellations?

Constellations are groups of stars that are situated relatively close to each other. Their distances are calculated by astronomers, who judge whether or not they form a pattern together. The constellations are then defined as patterns formed by the prominent stars known to us, on Earth. Some common constellations are Ursa Major and Ursa Minor. Another famous constellation is the Orion, which looks like the torso of a warrior.

28. What is Astronomy?

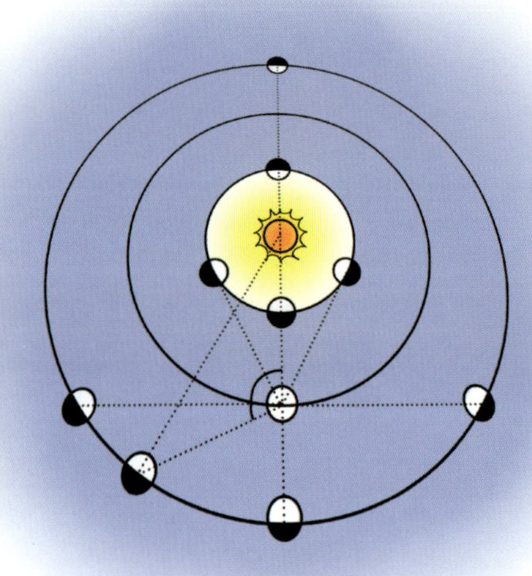

Astronomy is the science which studies celestial objects that lie beyond our Earth's atmosphere. It deals with planets, stars, constellations and other bodies. Astronomy has a rich history: the world's oldest civilisations made use of Astronomy to tell the position of stars and even predict the future! Today, Astronomy is also heavily used for scientific research, as it links with physics. Scientists study various aspects of the Universe, such as, ultraviolet, infrared, optical and radio waves, under the larger heading of Astronomy.

29. What is an Aurora?

An Aurora is a phenomenon that occurs in the Arctic and Antarctic regions, or the poles of the Earth. It is actually an electromagnetic phenomenon, where particles are charged at the polar regions. Because of their charge, these particles begin to glow. Thus, auroras cause the sky to glow in a fluorescent green or sometimes in a faint red colour in the polar regions. The name 'Aurora' comes from the name of the Roman Goddess of Dawn because the glow looks like an unusual sunrise. Auroras are also known as the northern lights.

30. How can we use the Sun's energy?

There are many ways in which we can use the Sun's energy. Indeed, this energy, also called solar energy, is very important. We know how pollution is spreading throughout the world and killing our environment. We should use more natural sources of energy, such as, solar energy, which do not cause pollution. Solar energy, because of its natural heat, can be used for heating purposes. Solar cookers and water heating are examples of this. Scientists have made solar cells that convert the Sun's light into electric energy, which is used in solar lamps and solar calculators.

1. Who was the first astronaut?

An astronaut is a person trained by a human spaceflight programme to travel in outer space. In Soviet Russia, however, the term Cosmonaut was used for people who went into space. Therefore, even though the first man in space was Yuri Gagarin (April 1961), the first Astronaut was Alan Shepard Jr. (May 1961), an American Navy Officer and pilot, who was trained by National Aeronautics and Space Administration (NASA). He later became the fifth person to walk on the Moon in 1971.

2. Who was the first person to go to space?

The first person in space was Soviet Cosmonaut Yuri A. Gagarin. On 12 April, 1961, the Russian cosmonaut Yuri Gagarin blasted off into orbit in the Vostok-1 spacecraft. He circled the Earth once at an altitude of 320 km (200 miles). This achievement made Gagarin an international hero. The first woman in space was Valentina Tereshkova, who travelled in Vostok-6 in June 16, 1961 and orbited the Earth for three days.

3. Why do astronauts need space suits?

Astronauts need to wear space suits whenever they leave a spacecraft as they are exposed to very low or acute sub-zero temperatures and high levels of radiation. In space, there is no air to breathe and no air pressure. The bulky pressurised space suit helps them breathe and move around in gravity-less space. Without the suit, the astronaut would burn from radiation and freeze due to cold. The suits have breathing apparatus attached to them and weighted down footwear. Wearing a spacesuit allows an astronaut to survive and work in space.

4. How do astronauts repair satellites?

Astronauts go directly to the satellite that is in need of repair. They go on what is called a 'space walk' when they step outside their spacecrafts, if the satellite is close enough. They usually have a line around their waists that is attached to the spacecraft to hold them. Carrying their tool boxes and using their tools carefully (if they do not hold on to them, the tools will drift away in gravity-less space), they fix what is possible in space itself. Sometimes astronauts visit orbiting satellites to check if these need maintenance and repair. Often they work using the space shuttle's robotic arms. They can also use manned units (a chair that acts as a vehicle) that are manoeuvrable and cover greater distances. If a lot of time is required for repairs, then the satellite can be pulled into the payload bay of the spacecraft, so they may work with ease.

5. Why do things float around in space?

There is weak or no gravity in outer space, so things have no weight or intended direction and keep floating slowly forever till they hit another object. Gravity is the force that pulls things down till they can go no further. Gravity gives weight to objects; in space an object or a body becomes weightless. The laws of motion state that a body at rest will remain at rest until a force acts upon it. Planets have a gravitational field that weakens as one goes further away. In space, the further one is away from the planets, the weaker the pull of gravity is. Floating objects in space could be affected by a planet, but only very slightly and they might be moving towards a planet or moving towards the Moon.

6. Has an animal ever been to space?

Yes, several animals have been sent into space. The first animals deliberately sent into space were fruit flies, sent by USA in February 1947, and they came back alive. Albert II, a rhesus monkey was sent in June 1949, and many monkeys and mice were sent in the 1950s and 1960s to check and monitor the conditions of survival before manned human flight was undertaken. In July 1951, the Russians sent the dogs, Tsygan and Desik, into space but not into orbit. In November 1957, Laika was sent into orbit but died aboard the spacecraft as the technology to return had not been developed. Able and Baker, two monkeys became the first animals to survive space flight in 1959. They travelled aboard an American spacecraft, Jupiter IRBM- AM 18. In August 1960, two dogs, Belka and Strelka, travelled to outer space and back aboard the Russian aircraft, Sputnik 5.

7. Who was the first person to land on the Moon?

On 28 July, 1969, Neil Armstrong, an American astronaut, was the first person to walk on the Moon. He was born on August 5, 1930. He first served in the US Navy as a test flight pilot. He then participated in the earliest US space programmes and joined the NASA Astronaut Corps in 1959. After his first spaceflight aboard the Gemini 8, he flew as mission commander of the Apollo 11 flight to the Moon, accompanied by Buzz Aldrin. "That's one small step for man, and one giant leap for mankind," were Armstrong's famous words as he stepped off the Apollo Lunar Module. He explored the Moon's surface for a few hours before returning.

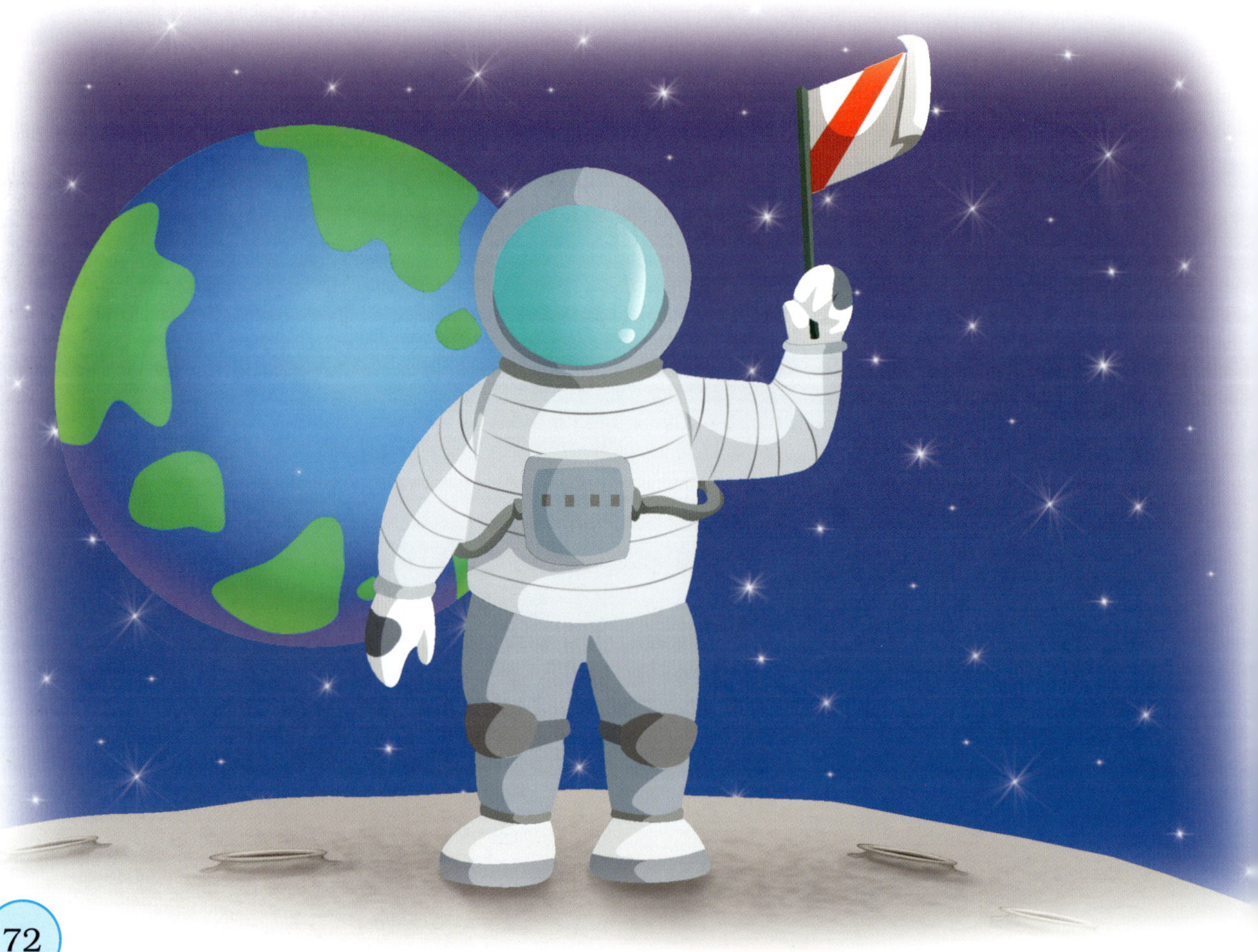

8. What can you see on the Moon?

The Moon has a powdery, dusty surface that is pockmarked with small and big craters (holes created due to the impact of meteorites). The surface is composed of rock that has been severely weathered. Many teams of astronauts and scientists have studied the Moon. There are basically two parts of the Moon—the maria or the plains, and the highlands or the rockier, higher areas. The giant crater on the far side is the most visible feature on the Moon, and is called the South Pole-Aitken basin. The near side of the Moon has dark patches of maria, while the far side is lighter in colour.

9. How long did it take to reach the Moon?

The Moon is 380, 000 kilometres away from the Earth. The first mission to the Moon, the Soviet Luna 1, took 36 hours to reach and fly by the Moon in 1959. The US Apollo 11 mission took 3 days, 3 hours and 49 minutes to reach lunar orbit. The fastest travel time into lunar orbit is 8 hours, recorded by the NASA's New Horizons Pluto mission, which was launched in 2006. The slowest trip was achieved by the ESA Smart 1 Lunar probe, launched in 2004.

10. Can people live in space?

Yes, people can live in space quite comfortably—in spacecrafts and in space stations, like the International Space Station. This particular station is a habitable, artificial satellite in low level Earth orbit (between 278 and 460 kilometres above the Earth). It is the eleventh space station, following the Salyut, Almaz, Cosmos, Skylab and Mir. These stations are well-pressurised with micro-gravity, designed for and adapted to human living conditions. It is also a research laboratory, where experiments are carried out. This space station is a joint project between American, Japanese, Canadian, European and Russian space agencies. People from 15 nations have visited this station.

11. What is Mission Control?

Mission Control or Mission Control Centre is a body that supports and manages aerospace flights at the ground level. When in flight, the communications between the spaceflight team and Earth are managed by flight controllers. The members of the Mission Control are technically trained staff dealing with all aspects of space craft and space flight. Mission Control Centres are also responsible for conducting training for these flights. Many rehearsals are carried out before the actual flight occurs. NASA's Mission Control Centre is located in Lyndon B. Johnson Centre in Houston and the Russian Mission Control centre is in Korolyov.

12. Which probe chased a comet?

The primary purpose of comet-chasing probes is to observe comets and to study how the comet changes over time. Several space probes have chased comets, including NASA's Stardust Spacecraft, launched in 1999 to collect dust and gas from around Comet Wild-2. Later, the European Space Agency launched the Rosetta interplanetary spacecraft on a 10-year journey in 2004. This is the first probe that will not only chase but also orbit and land on a comet.

13. Why is the Earth the only planet where humans live?

The Earth is the third planet in the Solar System. It is at a distance of about 93 million miles from the Sun. At this distance, it gets the accurate amount of heat and light from the Sun, not more and not less. The Earth has a dense core and is large enough to hold its atmosphere, unlike planets like Mars, where the air is very thin. Also, the Earth has large tracts of water on its surface. This is very important because life originated underwater!

14. What is a volcano?

A volcano is a mountain but it is very different from the mountains that we usually see. A volcano is formed when hot and molten matter from below the Earth's surface is pushed out in the open and it forms a conical structure on cooling. A vent is left open on the top from where the molten matter keeps pouring out.

15. What are magma and lava?

Our Earth has a lot of matter hidden beneath its surface. Moreover, with lots of pressure and heat, this matter is constantly changing its form. The molten rock and metal matter beneath the Earth's surface is called magma. When it flows out in hot streams from the volcano, it is known as lava.

16. Why do volcanoes erupt?

With intense heat and pressure inside the Earth, the rocks and metals melt and form the magma. With this a lot of gases like carbon dioxide and sulphur dioxide are also formed. This pushes the magma along with the gases out from the vent of the volcano, causing an eruption.

17. What does the Earth's surface consist of?

The Earth's surface is made up of land and water. However, most of our Earth is made up of water—almost 70 per cent! This means that if you put together all the countries and continents, they would only make up 30 per cent of the Earth's total surface area. The surface of land is actually made up of rock. Over it, various forms of soil and debris lie, which support the growth of plants and animals.

18. What lies beneath the Earth?

The Earth's surface or uppermost layer is known as the crust. It is made up of different kinds of rocks, mainly known as sedimentary, igneous and metamorphic rocks. This outermost layer is 5 to 70 kilometres thick and makes up for only 1 per cent of the Earth's total mass. Below the crust is a thick layer called the mantle. The mantle is also made of rocks, but these rocks are much denser than the ones we find on the crust. The outer layer of the mantle is known as the upper mantle. The entire mantle is about 2,890 kilometres deep and is the thickest layer. The innermost layer of the Earth is known as the core. It is also divided into two layers. The outer core is a liquid layer, made up of the elements iron and nickel. The inner core, on the other hand, is solid and dense. Scientists believe that it is mostly made up of iron. Our knowledge of the Earth's core is limited, because it is so deep down the surface.

19. What is a supernova?

Have you heard about a Supernova before? It is a term that is related with the stars that you see at night. When one of these stars explodes, it is known as a Supernova. So, a Supernova is actually an exploding star. When this happens, a star becomes much, much brighter. In fact, it can become billions of time brighter than even the Sun! In fact, when a Supernova is shining at its maximum capacity, it becomes brighter than an entire galaxy! However, once the explosion is over, a huge amount of dust and gas are shot into the space and the star that exploded disappears. Although scientists have not observed any Supernova in our Milky Way in more than 400 years, they have proof that Supernovae do happen once in every 50 years. Evidence also suggests that when a Supernova happens, the explosion sends shock waves through space. These shock waves help in the formation of new stars.

20. How old is the Earth?

There are varying beliefs regarding how old our Earth is. Scientists have tried to estimate the age of the Earth by a process called Radiometric Age Dating. In this method, the Earth's age has been calculated with the help of meteorite particles and lunar samples. According to this method, the Earth is extremely old, around 4.54 billion years old! Apart from this scientific view, there are also certain religious beliefs about the age of the Earth. Young Earth Creationists, for example, do not believe that the Earth was formed by some scientific process. According to them, our planet is relatively young—just around 6,000 to 10,000 years old.

21. How big is the Earth?

There are numerous ways to measure how large the Earth is—by size, diameter or weight. Water constitutes 70.8 per cent of the Earth's surface area. That means that a major portion of our Earth is taken up by oceans, seas, rivers and lakes! The remaining 29.2 per cent area is land. That means that all the countries and continents, when put together, form only a 29.2 per cent of the Earth! The Earth measures 24,850 miles around the equator and about 24,800 miles around the poles. And it weight almost 5,940,000,000,000,000,000,000 metric tons. Don't we live on a huge, huge planet!

22. How are mountains formed?

Mountains are formed in two broad ways. The first is when the Earth has crustal plates or tectonic plates under its surface. When crustal plates collide against each other, the surface of the Earth is pushed up to form high mountains. The second way in which mountains are formed is through volcanoes. When the tectonic plates move, molten magma is pushed upwards to the surface of the Earth. The lava and gases are also pushed upwards with great force. Such eruptions form mountains. This is the way in which most mountains are formed under the ocean.

23. Do mountains shrink?

As odd as it sounds, mountains really do shrink. Actually, there are forces that cause them to both grow and shrink at once. When crustal plates collide, they push the mountain upwards, causing it to grow. On the other hand, strong winds, rains and storms cause mountains to weather away and erode. This makes them shrink. Also, the force of the Earth's gravity pulls the mountains downwards, but very slowly. With the course of time, gravitational forces may completely pull a mountain downwards, causing it to go flat!

24. Why are some mountain-tops snowy?

As we travel to high mountains, the air becomes thinner and thinner. This thin air at great altitudes also has smaller portions of gases, such as, oxygen. It is for this reason that it is so cold at high altitudes and hill stations. Now, some mountains are so tall that at their peaks, the air is extremely cold all the time. This is why snow forms on such mountain peaks. Since it is so cold throughout the year in these places, the air never warms sufficiently for the snow to melt. Thus, some mountain-tops are snowy.

25. What is a snow avalanche?

A snow avalanche is a natural force, much like tornadoes, hailstorms and earthquakes. It begins with loose snow sliding down a slope. As this loose snow slides, it gathers more snow. Thus, it becomes larger, wider and more massive. A snow avalanche falls with varying speeds, depending on whether the snow it carries is dry, damp or wet. Avalanches with dry snow are the fastest ones, as the dry snow comes loose easily. In fact, particles of dry snow even form a cloud-like mass of snow dust in the air, around the avalanche. Thus, an avalanche of dry snow, along with sliding down a slope, also half-flies in the air!

26. What are the popular types of volcanoes?

Popularly, volcanoes are classified into three types—Active, Dormant or Inactive and Extinct. Active volcanoes are those that erupt regularly. Dormant or inactive volcanoes are those that have erupted in historical times but are asleep now. Extinct volcanoees are those that have not erupted even in historical times and are unlikely to.

27. Why is lava runny?

Some volcanoes house a kind of lava that is thinner than that found in others. Such lava is, thus, 'runny'. This is because such lava has low viscosity. Viscosity is a measure of how dense a liquid is. Thus, lower viscosity means that the liquid has low density and is, therefore, runny. Such runny lava forms 'shield volcanoes'. It has low viscosity because it has low silica content but is rich in minerals, such as magnesium and iron. Shield volcanoes have flat slopes and are not very explosive. You can easily find such volcanoes in Iceland and Hawaii.

28. Are earthquakes dangerous?

Earthquakes occur in varying degrees of intensity. The Richter Scale is a measure of how dangerous an earthquake is. Higher the Richter Scale measure, more dangerous an earthquake. Thus, though some earthquakes are mild, many are intense and may cause great destruction, because they cause the earth to shake so vigorously. This often causes buildings to fall. Such earthquakes may also lead to failure of electric grids, or cause short-circuits and fire. Also, if an earthquake originates in the ocean, it may even lead to a tsunami. This may further lead to landslides and loss of life and property. Although such dangerous earthquakes cannot be prevented, there are ways to be safe from them. Thus, we should learn the precautions and safety measures to remain unharmed from natural calamities.

29. Where do earthquakes happen?

Earthquakes mostly happen in those parts of the world that lie above the boundaries of tectonic plates. This is because earthquakes are caused when tectonic plates come together or move apart.

The areas along the boundaries of tectonic plates have been named as Earthquake Belts. The most earthquake-prone belt of the world is the Circum-Pacific belt, which lies along the Pacific Ocean. This belt runs along Chile, the South American coast, Central America, Mexico, the American West Coast, Southern Alaska, parts of Japan, the Philippine Islands, New Guinea, Southwest Pacific and New Zealand. Almost 81 per cent of the world's earthquakes occur in this belt.

Another Earthquake Belt is known as Alpide. It runs along Java, Sumatra, the Himalayas, the Mediterranean and the Atlantic. 17 per cent of the world's earthquakes occur in this area.

30. Are there mountains underwater?

Yes, there are mountains underwater. They are formed by tectonic activity, just as mountains are formed on land. Under water, a mountain is formed when continental plates collide together. Because of the collision, the edges of the continental plates push upwards and form a mountain. The largest mountain range of the world is actually an underwater mountain range! It is called the Mid-Atlantic Ridge and lies in the Atlantic Ocean. In fact, there are more mountains under water than on land!

31. Which is the deepest ocean point in the world?

The Challenger Deep in the Pacific Ocean is the deepest part of any ocean in the world. This point is located in the Marianas Trench near the island of Guam in the west Pacific. At 11 kilometres, this point is 2 kilometres deeper than Mount Everest's height! Challenger Deep is so named as it was the British survey ship *Challenger II*, which first noticed the deepest point in 1951.

1. Why is sea water salty?

Sea water is salty because of the combined presence of chemicals, mineral salts and decayed remains of marine animals. The main sources from where these minerals and chemicals get added to the sea include the rivers and streams that add water to the sea, rainfalls, weathering of the rocks below the sea and other minerals that flow into the sea after a volcanic eruption. Moreover, when the Sun shines brightly, pure water is evaporated from the sea, leaving concentrations of salt behind; making the sea water very salty.

2. What are river rapids?

Certain sections of a river bed have a steep gradient which causes turbulence in the water flowing over it. This is known as a rapid. Here the river becomes shallower and the rocks get exposed above the surface of the water flow. A rapid has a run and a cascade. Because of the rocks that the water hits on, air bubbles are formed and the water appears frothy, giving it an appearance of 'whitewater'.

3. What are estuaries?

An estuary is the section where a river meets the sea or ocean. This is where the fresh water from the river and the salt water from the sea mingle. Bays, and harbours are forms of estuaries. The land or coastal area that surrounds an estuary is actually salt marshes that are grassy and low lying. Estuaries form the point of transition for rivers, as they mingle with the sea or ocean, and this gives home to a variety of organisms.

4. Which rocks are made from shells?

Some kinds of rocks are actually made up of shells. Along with other matter, these shells are squeezed together under the sea and form a solid rock mass. These rocks are called Sedimentary Rocks. They are formed when shells and other debris are left squeezed together, or compressed, for long time spans. The pressure of the sea water forces the shells, seaweed and other oceanic material to compress. After many years, these shells and debris merge together to form rocks.

5. Where do rivers start?

The place where a river starts is known as its source. Rivers have their sources at places of altitude, usually mountains or hills. Water from rains and melting snow collects at these places. This pool of collected water then forms small streams that start flowing. When several streams merge together, a tributary is formed. Finally, when many flowing tributaries meet to form one large water body, a river is formed.

6. What is a water cycle?

The Water Cycle, also known as the Hydrologic Cycle, is the movement of water from the earth to the sky and back to the earth. This cyclical movement takes place through the processes of evaporation and condensation. Evaporation means the conversion of water into vapour from the surface of any kind of water body. Condensation is the opposite process, meaning conversion of vapour back into water. It is because of the Sun's heat that water from the surface of the oceans, seas, rivers and lakes evaporates and turns into vapour. This vapour then rises into our atmosphere. Here, the vapour cools and condenses back into water droplets. Such droplets combine together to form clouds. When too many droplets collect in a cloud, it becomes too heavy to stay high in the atmosphere. Thus, the water returns to the Earth as rainfall, dew and snowfall. This completes the Water Cycle.

7. How high are waterfalls?

Different waterfalls have different heights. The highest waterfall in the world is Angel Falls. It is located in Venezuela and is 3,212 feet or 979 metres high. That's almost twice as tall as the Empire State Building or the Burj Khalifa Towers in Dubai (a seven star hotel)! Angel Falls has a drop of 2,648 feet or 807 metres, deep, followed by sloped cascades and rapids. Other high waterfalls include the Waihilau Falls in Hawaii. This waterfall is 2,600 feet or 793 metres high. The Monge Falls in Norway is also extremely high, with a drop of 2,535 feet or 773 metres.

8. Which river carries the most water?

When measured by the amount of water a river carries, River Amazon is the largest river in the world. Every second, the mouth of this river pours out 120,000 cubic metres of water. This is equal to the amount of water 20 swimming pools contain! In terms of length, Amazon is the second longest river in the world.

9. What is a lake?

A lake comes under that category of water bodies that have standing water. This means that the water in such bodies is still and does not flow. More such water bodies include ponds, reservoirs, man-made lakes and so on. Natural lakes are formed due to certain processes of nature, such as, melting of glaciers, oxbows in rivers, and so on. Lakes form an important part of our environment, as they are the places where water from small streams collect. They also provide humans with water to drink and irrigate crops with, where there are no rivers.

10. Where is the world's biggest freshwater lake?

Lake Baikal is the largest freshwater lake in the world. It is located in Siberia, Russia. It is so large that even if we combine the water from all five of the North American Great Lakes, it would still not be sufficient to completely fill Lake Baikal! It is 1,620 metres deep. In terms of the amount of water it holds, Lake Baikal is the largest freshwater lake. In comparison, Lake Superior of the United States of America is the third largest freshwater lake. However, it has the largest surface area of all freshwater lakes of the world.

11. Which is the longest river?

The longest river in the world is River Nile. It is 6,695 kilometres long. It is the major north-flowing river in north-east Africa. The source of this river is in a place called Burundi. The two tributaries of the Nile are the White Nile and the Blue Nile. The White Nile is the longer tributary, while the Blue Nile is more fertile. The northern part of the river flows through Egypt. In ancient times, the Egyptian civilization developed around the River Nile.

12. How do rivers carve out valleys?

It is fascinating, really, that entire valleys can be made out of flowing water! Rivers usually flow out from high mountains. So, the intensity of their flow is extremely fast and fierce. This furious flow of water cuts at rocks, as it moves down the mountain. It also breaks away rocks in smaller pieces and eventually grinds those pieces into even smaller pieces of sediment. Thus, a deep and steep valley is formed, usually in a V-shape because of the river's course.

13. How are lakes formed?

Natural lakes are formed by natural processes. For example, tectonic activity underneath the Earth's surface may cause a bowl-like depression on the surface. This depression may then fill up with water from rainfall, snowfall or glacial activity. Thus, a natural lake is formed. In fact, lakes may also disappear naturally—when too much sand infiltrates a lake, it becomes a swamp or a marsh. Also, due to seasonal changes, a lake may dry up if it does not have enough water.

14. How big is the sea?

Seas are water bodies that are usually larger than lakes, ponds or rivers, but are smaller than the oceans. In fact, they mostly constitute a part of one ocean or the other. For example, the Arabian Sea and the Bay of Bengal are seas that are parts of the Indian Ocean. The largest sea in the world is the Mediterranean Sea. It has a total surface area of 1,144,800 square miles and it is connected to the Atlantic Ocean.

15. Which is the biggest ocean?

The biggest ocean in the world is the Pacific Ocean. It has an area of 165.2 million square kilometres and occupies more than 33 per cent of the Earth's entire surface area. In fact, the Pacific Ocean is larger than all the land areas of the world put together! Its boundaries extend from both the Americas to Asia and Australia on the other side.

16. Is an ocean the same as a sea?

No, oceans and seas are not the same. Although both are large water bodies and both contain salty water, there are some very important differences between the two. The primary distinction is that a sea usually makes up for only a part of an ocean. A sea is partly bound by land. Some seas are completely surrounded by land. Then, it is called an inland sea. An ocean, on the other hand, has no boundaries. This is why its volume cannot be measured. It is always larger than a sea. Mediterranean, Black, Arabian, Red and so on are seas, whereas Atlantic, Indian, Pacific and Arctic are oceans.

17. Why is the sea blue?

A sea appears blue because of two phenomena: reflection and refraction. When sunlight falls on the water's surface, a part of it is reflected, meaning the sunrays bounce back off the sea's surface. Thus, it acts like a mirror to the sky and looks blue. Secondly, some sunrays are refracted, meaning the rays bend as they hit the water. Light is made up of seven colours. When it refracts, the colour blue refracts the most. This, along with reflection, adds to the 'blueness' of the sea or ocean's surface. Hence, the water appears blue although it is actually colourless.

18. Where do waves come from?

Waves are basically the Sun's creation. Throughout the day, the Sun's heat energy warms the air. Since warm air is lighter in weight, it rises up above. As this happens, the heavier cold air takes its place below. When this cool wind blows near the ocean's surface to take up the warm air's space, it pushes the water, which rushes forward in the form of waves.

19. What causes the tide?

Large volumes of water rise and fall in seas and oceans daily—this phenomenon is known as a tide. Tides are caused because of the gravitational forces of the Moon. At night, the Moon's gravitational force pulls the water from the ocean towards itself. Thus, a large volume of water is attracted towards the Moon and a tide is caused. Tides are classified as high and low. A high tide, as the name suggests, is when the water rises up to a much higher level. During low tide, the gravitational pull of the Moon is not so strong. Tides generally change every twelve hours.

20. How does a coral reef grow?

At the initial stage of its life cycle, a coral is just a larva and is called a coral polyp. This larva floats around under water. On finding a proper location, it attaches itself there. The coral polyp then releases a chemical substance called limestone. This forms a hard outer protection for the tiny creatures. In addition, the minute cells of the corals protect them by stinging any creature that tries to eat them. Thus, a coral reef continues to grow.

21. Where is the biggest coral reef?

Coral reefs are typically found in tropical oceans, at or near the equatorial countries of the world. The biggest coral reef in the world is located in Australia and is known as the Great Barrier Reef. The second biggest coral reef is situated on the coast of Belize in Central America. Other famous reefs are located in Hawaii, the Red Sea and the seas of South-East Asia.

22. What are mermaids?

Mermaids are mythological creatures that do not actually exist. They are supposed to be females that live underwater and have the head and torso of a woman, but are fish-like from the waist-downwards. Mermaids are said to be very beautiful creatures and were very popular in folktales, mythology and fantasy literature. The famous cartoon character, Ariel, is also a mermaid!

23. What is a desert?

A desert is any region on Earth that has very low rainfall throughout the year. With less rainfall, the plants and animals in that region are also affected. Very few plants and trees survive in a hot and dry desert. In fact, the plants that do grow in deserts are short and thick as then they can store water. The animals remain burrowed deep in the sands to protect themselves from the heat. In a cold desert, snow and dry winds are experienced throughout the year. There is hardly any vegetation seen in such areas. The animals have a thick coat of fur on their bodies to face the chilly winds.

24. Which is the world's largest hot and dry desert?

The Sahara Desert in Northern Africa is the world's largest hot and dry desert. However, this desert is the second largest if we include the cold desert Antarctica. The Sahara covers most of North Africa and the sand dunes can reach heights of more than 500 feet!

25. How are deserts formed?

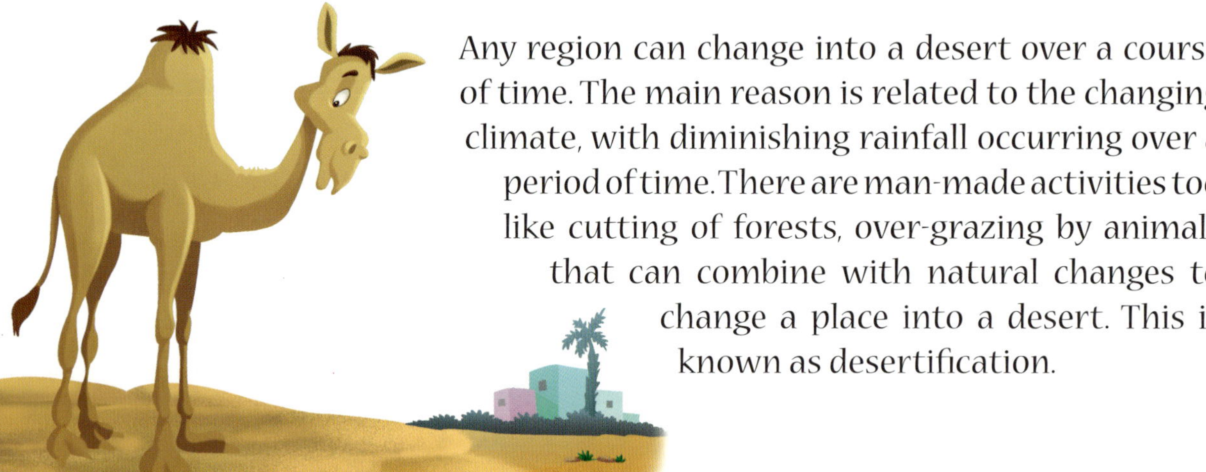

Any region can change into a desert over a course of time. The main reason is related to the changing climate, with diminishing rainfall occurring over a period of time. There are man-made activities too like cutting of forests, over-grazing by animals that can combine with natural changes to change a place into a desert. This is known as desertification.

26. Can camels live without water?

Camels can travel up to 161 kilometres without water! Camels have gifted bodies for the tough desert conditions. They rarely sweat in summers, lose less water in urine and have thick skinned coats that keep their bodies cool. When thirsty, camels can drink almost 135 litres of water in less than 15 minutes. This water swells up their red blood cells into an oval shape, unique to this species of mammals. These cells gradually keep the body hydrated.

27. Where is the biggest rainforest?

With the widest variety of vegetation and animal life, the Amazon Rainforest is the largest rainforest. Known as Amazonia, this rainforest covers areas in Brazil, Venezuela, Colombia, Ecuador and Peru. With thousands of trees, the Amazon Rainforest has been labelled as the 'Lungs of our Planet Earth'. More than 20 per cent of the world's oxygen is produced in the Amazon Rainforest.

28. How are rainforests useful?

Rainforests are one of the important ecosystems present on Earth. These ecosystems play an important part in converting carbon dioxide into useful oxygen for the living beings to breathe. The rainforests are an essential source of fruits, herbs, spices and nuts. In fact, some herbs and medicinal plants have proven to be very useful in developing medicines. Rainforests also support a variety of animal species, too.

29. What is a forest canopy?

Forest canopy is the top view of the tree cover formed by the tallest trees in a forest. Like an umbrella, it stops the sunlight from reaching the plants and trees at a lower height. The Amazon rainforests have a forest canopy as deep as 10 metres. Since sunlight does not reach below the forest surface, a wide variety of animals live on trees in rainforests.

30. Which is the world's smallest country?

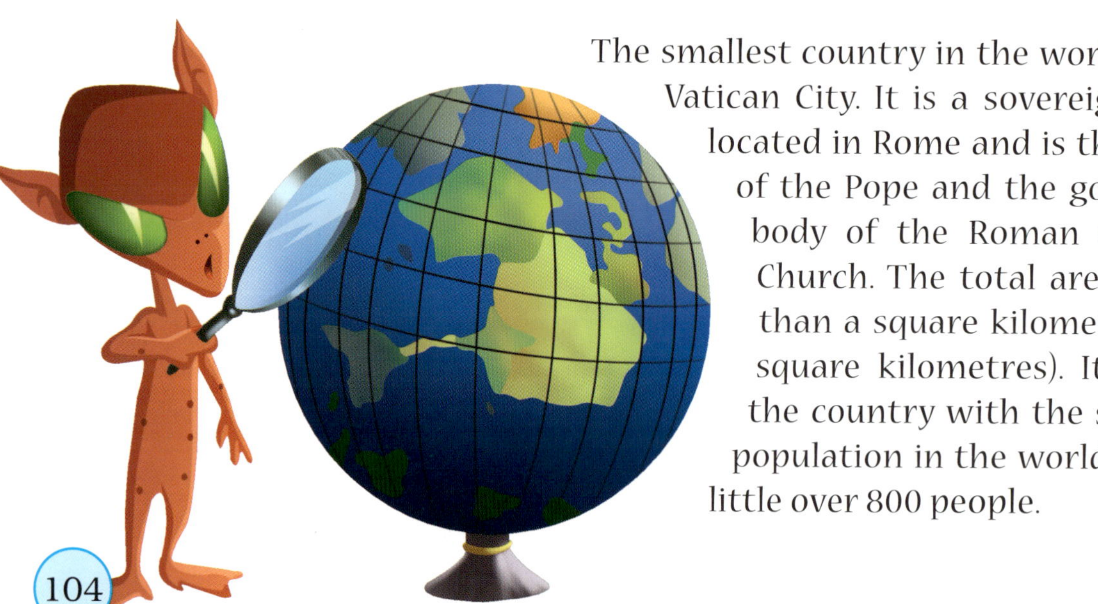

The smallest country in the world is the Vatican City. It is a sovereign state located in Rome and is the home of the Pope and the governing body of the Roman Catholic Church. The total area is less than a square kilometre (0.44 square kilometres). It is also the country with the smallest population in the world, with a little over 800 people.

1. Where in the world would you find the ring of fire?

We know that our Earth has a lot of hot matter inside its surface. Magma or molten rocks are the fieriest for they are constantly pushed out to the Earth's surface, causing the plates lying under the Earth's surface to collide or move. This causes earthquakes and volcanic eruptions. Most of this activity occurs under the surface of the Pacific Ocean, extending from New Zealand, along the eastern edge of Asia, north across the Aleutian Islands of Alaska and south along the coast of North and South America. This region, called the Ring of Fire, witnesses 75 per cent of the world's active and dormant volcanoes and earthquakes.

urasian
Plate

Pacific
Plate

Ring Of Fire

Indo-Australian
Plate

Nazca
Plate

South
American
Plate

2. Is the North Pole an island?

An island is a land body that is covered with water from all sides. Until now, the North Pole was considered to be the northernmost tip of the world. However, with changing climatic conditions, the ice in the Artic Ocean has melted. Satellite images have shown that passages from Northwest over Canada and Northeast over Russia are now free of ice, making it possible to sail around the North Pole. Thus, it can be called an island now.

3. Which is the biggest island?

Any area of land that is completely surrounded by water is an island. Technically, Australia is an island, but it is so huge that it has been named as an entire continent in itself. So, after Australia, the world's largest island is Greenland. It has an area of 840,000 square miles or 2,175,590 kilometres. Greenland is situated close to the North Pole between North America and Europe. Thus, it is extremely cold there. In fact, more than 80 per cent of Greenland is occupied by glaciers, many of which are more than one kilometre thick. Very few people live in Greenland because of the extremely cold climate.

4. How are islands made?

There are two kinds of islands—continental islands and oceanic islands. They are named so because of the difference in the manner in which they were formed. Continental islands are basically extensions of a continent that remain connected underwater along the parent continent's coastline. Otherwise, the sea's activity may detach a land mass from its parent continent. Great Britain and Japan are continental islands. Oceanic islands are formed when volcanic activity or other disturbances take place on the ocean floor. Thus, such islands push out of the ocean floor. The islands of Hawaii are examples of oceanic islands.

5. Where does oil come from ?

Oil is formed by a very lengthy and slow process. Essentially, it comes from the remains of dead animals and plants that lived under the sea. Millions of years ago, when such sea animals and plants died, their remains were buried under many layers of earth. Over the years, these layers became thicker and thicker. In this way, these layers put immense pressure and heat over the remains. Very slowly, the tremendous heat and pressure converted the remains of living beings into crude oil. This crude oil is later refined by man-made processes and turned into oil that we use in our cars and for cooking. Indeed, the very word 'petroleum' literally means 'rock oil', or 'oil from the earth'.

6. Is the arctic region too cold for animals?

The Arctic is not too cold for animals. Wildlife does exist in these regions, but the animals have adapted to survive in the extremely cold temperatures. Examples of some animals that live in the Arctic Zone are the caribou, lemming, musk oxen, arctic foxes and wolves, and polar bears. These animals have thick, furry coats that keep them warm in the cold. Also, aquatic species, such as Arctic char, trout, grayling, walruses and whales may be found in the Arctic Ocean. These aquatic animals also have a thick layer of fat beneath their skins. This layer is called blubber and it adds to their warmth. The fish in the Arctic Ocean have a natural system that makes anti-freeze protein. This protein prevents their blood from freezing in the extremely cold water.

7. Can fish see in the dark?

The deeper we go into an ocean, the darker it becomes. This happens as sunlight is not able to penetrate beyond a few hundred metres below water. Despite this feature, the ocean is full of marine life. Most deep sea fish have large eyes that are adapted to see in the dark. Some species of fish have tentacles attached to their bodies that help them locate prey. A lateral line, which is a row of tiny holes, runs from behind the gills to the tail on a fish's body. It helps the fish in feeling movements in the water.

8. Which is the fastest fish?

The Sailfish can reach a speed of 110 kilometres per hour. Thus, it definitely has to be the fastest fish in the world. The Sailfish, with its amazing speed in water, is also very huge in size. It can grow up to 10 feet in length and weigh around 65 kilograms.

9. Which is one of the most dangerous sea creatures?

The Box Jellyfish is recognised as one the most dangerous marine creatures. Also known as sea wasps, these look like transparent and wobbly jelly and are found in coastal areas. With more than 50 tentacles, which reach a length of 10 metres, it can weigh up to 2 kilograms. Strangely, this creature does not hunt intentionally. But when humans bump into it accidentally, they face the harshest of the stings. The venom produced by the tentacles is poisonous enough to attack the heart, nervous system and skin cells. Interestingly, sea turtles are unaffected by the sting of the Jellyfish and instead eat them!

10. Which is the biggest sea mammal?

The largest known mammal on earth is the blue whale (*Balaenoptera musculus*). It belongs to the order *Cetacea*. Mature blue whales can measure anywhere from 75 feet (23 m) to 100 feet (30.5 m) from head to tail, and can weigh as much as 150 tons (136 metric tons). The largest whale measured so far was 110 feet long and weighed 200 tons. This group has a large set of dental plates called baleen in its mouth through which it filters its food. They also have extremely powerful back muscles which help them swim and navigate.

11. What special features help whales live in the sea?

Whales are warm-blooded mammals that nurse their young ones. They are well adapted to their marine environment. They have a thick layer of fat or blubber under their skin that insulates them and provides them with energy. They are able to process fat to extract water. All this enables them to survive icy temperatures. They also have special kind of teeth that help them get food easily. Their bodies are shaped (fusiform) in a way that facilitates easy movement in water. They have paddle-shaped fins in the top part and flukes (a divided flat tail) in the bottom part of their bodies. This helps them move vertically as well as horizontally. They breathe through blowholes that are located at the top of their heads. They can, thus, breathe underwater. Their ears are located a little beyond the throat cavity. They receive sound through their throats.

12. Do all whales have teeth?

There are basically two types of whales—baleen and toothed whales. The baleen whales have long, plate-like teeth, which look like the teeth on combs. The Sperm and Killer (Orcas) whales have teeth set in their jaws. Sperm whales only have teeth (50 in number) in their lower jaws. Humpback and Blue whales scoop large amounts of water and filter out their food (mainly krill) inside their mouths. Toothed whales use echolocation to locate their food and eat plankton and larger animals.

13. Which mammal can swim the fastest?

The fastest mammal in the water is supposed to be the Killer Whale or the *Orsinus orca*. It actually belongs to the oceanic dolphin family. It is supposed to attain speeds of up to 48 miles per hour (77 km per hour). These whales are found in the Arctic and Antarctic and tropical marine environments. These whales typically have black backs, white chest and sides and a white eye-patch above and below the eyes.

14. Why do whales sing to each other?

Marine animals that live underwater have a greater dependency on sound rather than sight. Since sound travels four times faster in water than it does in air, their sound and communication systems are highly effective. Whales communicate with each other even over long distances by using a series of sounds—hums, moans, tonal sounds, grunts, clicks and repeated sounds. Some of these sounds are highly melodious, regular and predictable and are called 'whale song'. Different species have different sounds and will vocalise in different situations. The humpback whale will only sing on calving and mating rounds. A single population has a similar song. Sperm whales use clicks to organise their food location activities. Toothed whales are known to use 'echolocation', a sound technique that can generate up to 20,000 watts of sound to locate their prey.

15. Which sea mammals live the longest?

Bowhead whales (*Baleana mysticetus*) or the Greenland or Arctic whales, found only in the Arctic and sub-arctic waters. These are considered to be the longest living mammals. In 2007, a whale was killed and a harpoon was found embedded in its neck blubber. This harpoon had been made in 1890. It was over a hundred years old. The oldest whale was 211 years old at the time of its death. They can grow to a length of 66 feet and weigh up to 75 tons. It is the largest among all animals, has the thickest blubber (17–20 inches) among all whales and is a social animal.

16. What are sharks?

Sharks are fish with a cartilaginous skeleton and highly streamlined body. They mostly inhabit warm water regions in seas and oceans. It is believed that sharks have existed for roughly 400 million years, even before dinosaurs came to live on Earth. There are 440 different species of sharks with the smallest being Dwarf Lantern Shark and the largest being the Whale Shark. The smallest shark is 17 centimetres in length and the largest is 12 meters long. Sharks are known to be at the top in the food cycle of marine animals and usually inhabit the deeper parts of the sea, as deep as 2000 metres (6,600 feet) under water. Most sharks have an upper grey body and bottom white surface. The dual shades help a shark to camouflage itself. Some sharks, such as, Bull Shark and River Shark can be found to inhabit seawater and freshwater. Although, we humans fear sharks, for they can attack us and kills us, they face more danger at our hands.

17. How old are sharks?

Little is known about the actual life span of sharks but different species live up to different number of years. The Great White Shark is said to live for 100 years and the Whale Shark is believed to live for 100-150 years. A Tiger Shark's life span is believed to extend between 30 to 40 years and approximately 25 years for a Nurse Shark.

The age of a shark can be determined by counting the number of circles on its backbone or the vertebrae. This is the way age is also calculated in trees by counting the number of concentric circles on a tree trunk. Sharks continue to grow throughout their life but their growth slows down after they reach maturity.

18. How fast can sharks swim?

Sharks are known to swim at a leisurely pace but Shortfin Mako is the fastest of all sharks. It is known to sprint across the ocean at a speed of 50 kilometres per hour and during moments of active burst at 74 kilometres per hour. The streamlined body of the Shortfin Shark, its pointed snout, large eyes and a tail supported by keel help it to swim swiftly. On the contrary, larger species of sharks have been observed to swim slowly at a speed of 1.5 kilometres per hour.

19. Why do sharks have a darker surface on the top?

The dorsal or the upper side of a shark is of darker colour and the ventral or lower side is of lighter shade. This colour coding helps the shark to camouflage itself with its surroundings and hide from predators. When sharks rest at the bottom of the sea their upper dark side blends with the dark water and when they swim to the top their bottom white merges with the light from top. As a result, both predators and prey cannot identify the shark amidst its surroundings.

20. Which is the biggest fish in the world?

The largest fish is the Whale Shark. It is 12 metres in length and weighs roughly 36 tons. Some studies suggest that some Whale Sharks are as long as 15-18 feet but these figures have not yet been confirmed. It has a long life and is said to live for 100 to 150 years. Whale Sharks are believed to have originated 60 million years ago and live in topical and warm areas of the sea. They are famous for their large mouths, which when open, look like a cave. They feed on planktons, microscopic plants and other animals. Whale Sharks are of a migratory nature. Every spring they migrate to the Continental Shelf of the West Coast of Australia.

21. What is the devil fish?

A Devil Fish is a giant Devil Ray and is bigger than the Lesser Devil Ray. It belongs to the family of myliobatidae and is species of the Eagle Ray. They are found in the Mediterranean Sea and Eastern Atlantic Ocean. It is approximately 200 inches in length and characterised by its spiny tail. The Devil Fish is called so because of its large size, which makes it look quite frightening. It has a large mouth and head, a single elongated dorsal fin and a rounded tail fin. Some Devil Fish can be very colourful but primarily they have a darker upper body and a lighter lower body, just like the sharks. They eat crustaceans, planktons and prey on small schools of fish for food. The Devil Fish is very sensitive to environmental changes and the pollution of the Mediterranean Sea and presence of fishing equipment's makes them aggressive.

22. Which is the biggest seal?

Seals are large mammals that live both on land and in water. Of all the different species of seals, the Elephant Seal is the largest. The Elephant Seal are further divided into two categories – Northern Elephant Seal and Southern Elephant Seal. The Southern Elephant Seals are larger than the Northern Elephant Seals and have a wider proboscis (trunk). Although the Southern Seals are the biggest, the male and female seals differ vastly in their size and weight. An average female weighs between 400-900 kilograms and is 2.3 to 3 metres long and an average male weighs 2,200-4000 kilograms and is 4.2 to 5 metres long. As per records, the largest seal was measured to be 6.85 metres in length and 5000 kilograms in weight in 1913, Possession Bay, South Georgia.

23. How do fish breathe?

Most fish breathe through gills. These are small organs, made of thread-like structures called filaments, located on both sides of the throat passage or pharynx. The gill opening is covered with a bony structure called an operculum. They breathe by swallowing water, which they pump into their gills. When the water rushes in, the capillaries in the gills absorb all the oxygen and the carbon-dioxide passes into the water going out. Some of the larger fish, like sharks have many gills, but have poor water pumping capacity. Therefore, they have to keep moving so that water automatically passes in and out of their gills.

Some fish, like the labyrinth fish have another breathing apparatus (labyrinth organ) above the gills that extracts oxygen from the air. The air-breathing fish breathe by coming to the surface from time to time, and use their gills when under water. Catfish absorb air through their digestive tracts, while some eels absorb oxygen directly through their skins, and lungfish breathe in air through their lungs and pass it out through their gills.

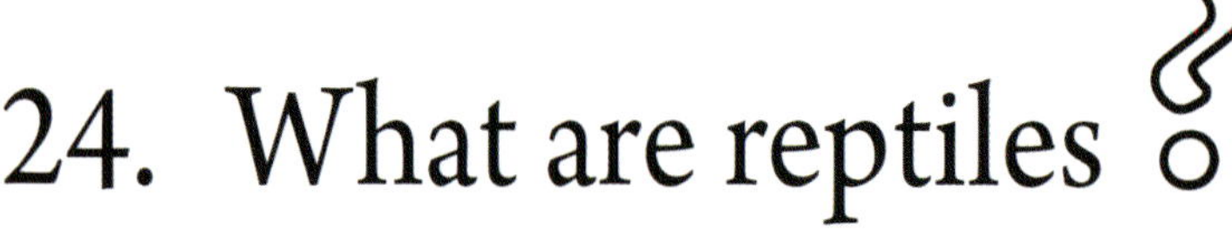

24. What are reptiles?

Reptiles are cold-blooded (ectothermic) vertebrates that breathe air. All ectothermic animals cannot produce body heat from within. They depend upon external sources of heat, such as the Sun, to keep themselves warm. All reptiles reproduce by laying eggs and snakes often feed themselves on the eggs of other animals. Reptiles do not have a slimy skin as we all think. Their skin is made up of hard scales, which protects their skin form drying out. The scales of a lizard are made of a protein called keratin that we can find in our hair and nails, too. Snakes, lizards, crocodiles and tortoise are all examples of reptiles. Reptiles are found everywhere in the world except Antarctica where they cannot survive because of cold weather.

25. Which is the shortest snake?

The Thread Snakes, as their name suggests, are the world's shortest snakes. There are 60 different species of the Thread Snake. Leptotyphlops Bilineata is the smallest of them all. This particular species of snake if found in the Caribbean at Martinique, Barbados and St. Lucia. The longest specimen of this snake has been measured to reach 10.8 centimetres (4.5 inches) long. It was so thin that it could enter the hole of the pencil whose lead had been removed.

26. What is the Ornate Tree Lizard?

Ornate Tree Lizards belong to the reptile family. Their scientific name is *Urosaurus ornatus*. This lizard species is native to the southwestern American region. The males of the species come in a variety of colours – almost as many as nine hues. They are known to change colour in reaction to their hormones. These lizards are highly aggressive and territorial. The males guard groups of as many as four female lizards. They mostly inhabit areas with large trees or a profusion of shrubs.

The females of the species lay batches of eggs, sometimes as many as three batches together. The males are nomadic in nature.

27. Which is the most poisonous land snake?

The most poisonous land snake is the Inland Taipan also referred to as the Small-scaled Snake or the Fierce Snake. Contrary to what the term 'Fierce' suggests, the snake is not aggressive by nature. It is a very shy animal and attacks only when threatened. It has been studied that 110 milligrams of Inland Taipan's poison can kill 100 humans and 250,000 rats. The Inland Taipan attacks its prey and then retreats backwards waiting for it to die under the effect of its venom. Only when the prey dies, does the snake consume it. The Inland Taipan can be found in dark shades of brown olive-green with its head and neck in a glossy black colour in winter and brown in summer. The Inland Taipan can warm itself by exposing just its dark head and neck to the sun. It preys on rats, rodents, small mammals and birds.

28. Which snake spits poison?

A snake that spits poison is the Spitting Cobra. However, the snake does not simply spit venom but sprays it in a particular pattern from the venom glands. The snake is known to be able to take a precise aim at the victim's eyes and spit venom in them. Also, it spits venom not to catch a prey but to protect itself from the predators. A Spit Snake can spray venom up to a distance of 2 metres. The venom of a Spit Snake is harmless if it touches the skin but can lead to permanent blindness if it comes in contact with the eyes. A spit can be found in different colours and patterns.

29. Why do snakes have elastic jaws?

Our upper and lower jaws are hooked with each other at the back of our mouths, but the jaws of snakes are joined together with elastic ligaments. Since these ligaments are flexible and placed far behind in its head, a snake can eat a prey that is many times larger than its head. The lower jaw of a snake does not have bones fixed in each other; rather these bones can move laterally and assist the snake in swallowing its prey. Also, there is a tube in the snakes' mouth that comes out far enough at the bottom of their mouths. This helps them breathe when their mouth swallows the prey.

30. Which lizard runs the fastest?

The Black Spiny-tailed Iguana also known as the Black Iguana or Black Ctenosaur found in Mexico and Central America is the fastest running lizard. These lizards can run at a speed of 34.9 kilometres per hour. The male lizards can grow to a length of 5 feet and females to 3 feet. Besides running fast to hide themselves from predators, these lizards can also whip their enemies with their tail and bite in retaliation. In Central America, they are called the 'chicken of the trees' and many people keep them as pets.

31. Can snakes climb trees?

Yes, snakes can climb trees in search of food and some stay on trees as their primary habitat. The Yellow Rat Snake is the best tree-climber and is found in Florida. The Brown Tree Snake, a nocturnal animal, is a popular species found in Papua, New Guinea and Australia. Its favourite habitat is at elevations of 1200 metres, in trees and in caves. Black Racer, a snake found mostly near water, is also a good tree climber. It eats rats and mice and can be easily found in areas inhabited by humans. There are also flying snakes that live on trees. These snakes do not have wings, but they can glide in the air from one tree to another.

1. How well can snakes hear?

For long, people believed that snakes have no ears and they cannot hear. But the theory is false! Snakes do not have ears like us humans but they do have an internal ear structure. When anything moves close to them, the vibrations caused by such movements reach them. The snakes then absorb these vibrations through their skin and muscles and take them to their internal ear structure. New researches have revealed that snakes can even hear sound waves that are carried through air. Through vibrations and sound waves, snakes can guess the distance at which their enemy or prey is located.

2. Which reptiles can look in two directions at the same time?

Chameleons, which are actually a specialised category of lizards, can look in two different directions at the same time. The upper and lower eyelids of a chameleon are joined together in a complete circle and the opening of the pupil is only as big as a pinhole. Although tiny, the gap is enough for the chameleon to take a quick look at its surroundings. It can rotate each eye in a different direction and focus each one at a different spot and thus obtain a 360-degree view of things around him.

3. Which is the longest snake?

There are many large snakes but the longest snake recorded till date was 11.5 metres long. It was a Green Anaconda and its likes can be found in the Amazon basin and Trinidad in South America. However, there is a dispute over the length of this snake. Some other researchers claim that the snake was no longer than 9 or 9.5 meters. An average Green Anaconda measures 15 to 28 feet. A green Anaconda has an olive-green skin marked with black spots. They are non-poisonous snakes and kill their prey by wrapping their huge body around it and suffocating it. They can also swim in water and feed on fish, reptiles, mammals and birds.

4. Which is the biggest lizard?

The Komodo Dragon found only in a few Indonesian islands is the biggest lizard and weighing 300 kilograms and stretching to ten feet (3 metres) in length. The amusing fact is that humans came to know of their existence only since the last 100 years. The Komodo Dragons are known for their patient way of hunting. They lay in ambush till their prey comes within their reach and then, using their powerful legs, sharp claws and teeth, they tear their prey apart. The bite of a Komodo Dragon is poisonous and it kills the prey because of blood poisoning within twenty-four hours of being bitten.

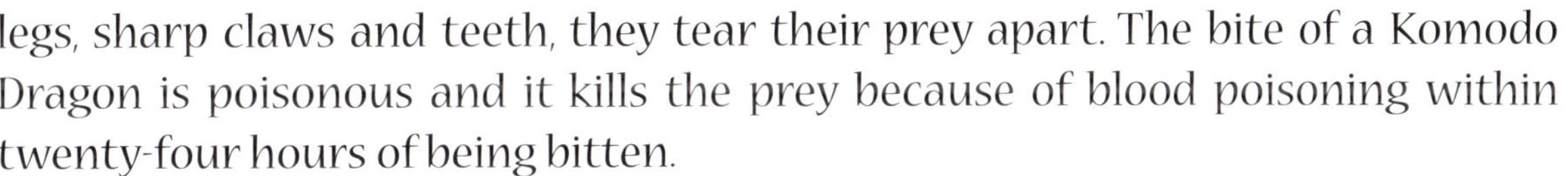

5. Which is the smallest lizard?

Only 16 millimetres long, *Sphaerodactylus Ariasae* is the smallest lizard in the word. The lizard was first found on the Caribbean Island off the coast of Dominican Republic. Not only is it the smallest lizard, but also the smallest species among the 23,000 different species of reptiles, birds and mammals

6. Which animals do not have spines?

Invertebrate animals do not have a spine or a backbone. Almost 97 per cent of all animals are invertebrates. This category of animals is quite large, ranging from small worms, snails and insects to the larger jellyfish and other marine creatures. All of them have soft bodies and are cold-blooded. Some of them have shells covering their bodies. The *Echinodermata* or the starfish, sea urchins and sea cucumbers live only in the seas and oceans. The Molluscs or snails, clams, nudibranchs and squids, and the Annelida or earthworms and leeches, are also other branches. The Arthropod branch includes insects, spiders and crabs. The Porifera or invertebrates such as the sponges is another branch. Most of them have highly flexible, soft bodies that allow them to move easily in the water. Platyhelminthes are the flatworms and Nematodes are the roundworms. Since they are all cold-blooded, their body temperature is always the same as that of their surroundings—on ground or in water, allowing them to survive in cold, humid and hot conditions.

7. Which is the biggest boneless creature?

The biggest boneless creature is the giant or colossal squid—*Mesonychotheuthishamiltoni*. It is also called the Antarctic or Giant Cranch Squid. Its body is 26 feet long and its tentacles are longer than its body. It has the largest eyes (30-40 centimetres across) in the animal kingdom. It can weigh up to 495 kilograms or more. Its limbs have sharp hooks at their ends. It eats other marine creatures and its body glows, enabling it to see its prey and find its way in the deep, dark waters. Adult colossal squids can live in depths of more than 7000 feet. This squid is found in an area of several thousand miles from the Antarctic to southern South America, southern South Africa and the southern tip of New Zealand—the entire southern ocean.

8. Do worms have skeletons?

Worms do not possess skeletons. They have rounded or flattened bodies. Some of them may also have a segmented body. They breathe through their skin. They do not have backbones and their bodies are very soft, with no hard outer cover. Some have a cavity in the body that supports certain basic body functions. There are different categories of worms (flatworms, roundworms) and they occupy land, marine and freshwater habitats. Worms have a hydrostatic body, which means that their bodies are mainly filled with fluid. They squeeze the muscles in one part of their body and the fluid goes into the relaxed part of the body ahead, pushing them in the same direction. They move in this way, using their circular and longitudinal muscles to control their movement.

9. Can insects fly?

Yes, many of those insects that have wings can fly—flies, bees, wasps, moths, butterflies, beetles, and dragonflies, to name a few. Some insects, such as ants, cannot fly. However, some ants are born with wings which they use for a day or so and then shed. The insects with two or four wings use their wings to fly. They flap their wings together, flying and changing their direction as they wish.

10. Why are frogs slimy?

Frogs have a protective layer of mucus on their skins that feels slimy to touch. This helps them retain the minimum level of moisture necessary to protect their delicate skin and survive. Frogs are amphibians. Animals that can live in water and on land are called amphibians. When they are in the water, this mucus layer acts as a waterproof coat, to prevent excessive wetness. The slippery skin also makes it difficult for predators to catch them.

11. How can you tell a frog from a toad?

It is easy to tell a frog apart from a toad. Toads have dry skins with bumps or warts all over it. Frogs have smooth and slimy skins. Toads have shorter bodies and legs than frogs. Frogs have longer legs and their back feet are webbed, unlike toads. Toads' eyes are set deeper in their faces, whereas frogs' eyes protrude or bulge out. Frogs lay eggs in clusters, whereas toads' eggs will be found in a long chain. However, it is important to remember that both frogs and toads belong to the same family, and sometimes you could find a warty frog or a slimy toad!

12. How long do tortoise live?

The giant tortoise live the longest amongst all the tortoise. Tortoise are reptiles belonging to the order of turtles and live on land, whereas turtles live in water. Usually, tortoise have a long life span as compared to other animals, living from 40 to over 200 years. The large tortoise found in the Galapagos Islands can live for more than 200 years. A tortoise called Tui Malila, born in 1777, presented by Captain Cook, the British explorer to the Tongan royal family, died on May 19, 1965! Another tortoise called Advaita, an Aldabra Giant Tortoise was said to be over 250 years old, when it died in Alipore Zoo in 2006.

13. Which are the tiniest animals?

If Amoeba were considered to be full-fledged animals, then these would be the smallest animals. However, since amoeba are considered as proto-animals, the Male Parasitic Wasp is the smallest animal in the world—just 139 micrometres in length. The next is a Nanosellini beetle, which is 300 micrometres long. A fish species, the Stout Infant in the Great Barrier Reef is 7 millimetres long, followed by the Brazilian Golden Frog that is between 9-10 millimetres long. The Dwarf Gecko is 16 millimetres long, the Bumblebee bat is 3-4 centimetres and the Bee Hummingbird is around 5 centimetres long. The smallest dog is the Chihuahua (12.4 centimetres), the smallest snake (*Leptotyphlopscarlae*) is as thin as a spaghetti noodle, at 10.1 centimetres. The smallest cat is 15.5 centimetres tall and 49 centimetres long and can fit into a glass.

14. Why are zebra striped?

The zebra's body has stripes to protect them from their predators. Stripes tend to be vertical across the head, neck, forequarters and main body with horizontal stripes on the legs and rear end. When standing in a herd, the jumble of black and white stripes makes it difficult to focus on one zebra. Hence the stripes are a good camouflage. Colour-blind animals such as lions confuse the stripes with the tall, savannah grass.

15. Which animal wears two fur coats?

The stoat, a type of weasel living in the Arctic, has two fur coats—its summer and winter coats. In summer, it has a brown coat that helps it blend with the surrounding and be safe from predators. In winter, it sheds its summer coat and grows thick, white fur to blend in with the snow. The white winter coat is also known as 'ermine'.

16. Why do rabbits have big ears?

Rabbits have big, long ears so the hearing surface in enhanced. This makes it easy for them to hear even very low sounds. When they are listening, their ears stand up and they receive the slightest sound at even long distances. They have few self-defence capabilities, so they rely mostly on their ears. When a rabbit's ears are upright, it is alert and ready to move quickly. If the ears are close to their head and they are lying flat on the ground, they are hiding from danger. The large ears also help the rabbit to cool down and regulate body temperature. The ear membrane is extremely thin with a network of blood vessels. If the ears are open, these blood vessels will cool down faster. Rabbits found in hotter environments usually have larger ears than their cousins in colder places.

17. What are tigers?

Tigers (*Pantheratigris*) are carnivorous, animals belonging to the cat species. Tigers grow to about 3.3 metres long, weigh about 306 kilograms, and have canines (teeth) at least 2.93 inches long. They have dark vertical stripes on reddish-orange fur with lighter coloured under-parts. Mutation can cause tigers to be white or a golden strawberry colour (golden tabby tiger). Once they were found all over Asia, from Turkey to eastern Russia. Now, they are can be found only in Siberian grasslands and certain parts of Asia, in open grasslands and mangrove swamps. The Bengal, Indochinese, Malayan, Sumatran and Siberian are the main species of tiger found today. The Bali, Javan and Caspian tigers are now extinct. Breeding tigers with lions has been successful and their offspring are called Ligers or Tigons.

Due to environmental change, habitat destruction and excessive hunting and poaching, tigers are in danger of being extinct, unless protected. They require large habitats which support their prey, and often clash with humans. They also live in areas of dense human population, which has an adverse effect on them. They live to be at least 25 years. The Royal Bengal Tiger is the national animal of both India and Bangladesh.

18. Which is the fastest animal on land?

The fastest animal on land is the Cheetah, which can run at a speed of 70 miles per hour (mph). The Cheetah belongs to the cat family and is found in most parts of Africa and also in the Middle East. The next fastest animal is the Pronghorn Antelope, found in North America, which can achieve speeds up to 61 mph. The fastest speed recorded for man is about 25 mph; while racehorses can run as fast as 50 mph.

19. How many kinds of tigers are there?

There are various types of tigers in different parts of the world. These belong to the species *Panthera tigris*. The *Panthera tigris tigris* (in Bangladesh, Bhutan, India, Burma, Nepal), the *Panthera tigris altaica* (China, Korea, Russia), the *Panthera tigris amoyensis* (in China), the *Panthera tigris sumatraea* (in Indonesia), and *Panthera tigris corbetti* (Cambodia, Laos, Burma, Thailand, Vietnam) and the known tiger varieties. In 1900, after a worldwide census, it was established that there were over 100,000 tigers alive. In 1950, there were 40,000 tigers but today, there are between 6000 to 9000 tigers left. In India, the tiger population was recorded as numbering 1706 in the 2010 census.

20. Which is the biggest dog?

The biggest dogs ideally are the Saint Bernard, followed closely by English Mastiffs. The Neapolitan Mastiff, Newfoundland, French Mastiff, Great Dane, Irish Wolfhound, Presa Canario, Pyrenean mountain dog and the Kuvasz are the ten largest dogs, in the order given.

The Guinness Book of World Records declared in June 2011, that George, the Great Dane, was officially the largest dog. He is 43 inches high and weighs 252 pounds. In June 2001, Hercules, an English mastiff was said to be the largest dog. His neck measured 38 inches and he weighed 282 pounds.

The tallest dog in the world was Gibson. He was a harlequin Great Dane who stood 7 feet tall on his hind legs. The heaviest dog was Kell, an English Mastiff who weighed 286 pounds in 1999 when he was two years old. Then there was Moose, an English Mastiff who weighed 291 pounds. However, in 1989, an English Mastiff, Zorba, set a record by weighing 343 pounds at the age of eight.

21. Which is the biggest bear?

All bears are large animals but the polar *(Ursus maritimus)* and brown *(Ursus arctos)* bears are among the largest. To be specific, it is the Kodiak brown bear *(Ursus arctos middendorffi)*. It can weigh up to 2,500 pounds and is between 7 and 10 feet long. The polar bear can weigh up to 2,200 pounds and is around 8 feet in length. The other living species are the American Black Bear, the Asiatic Black Bear, the Giant Panda, the Sloth Bear, the Sun Bear and the Spectacled Bear. If we look at the prehistoric record, we find that there once existed a 'South American Giant Short-faced Bear'. It would have weighed around 3,500 pounds and would have been 11 feet high when standing.

22. What is the difference between a monkey and an ape?

Monkeys and apes both belong to the family of primates and have the same ancestors. But as evolution started the primates divided themselves into two groups. One group evolved as apes and the other as monkeys. We humans come in the category of apes. Others in the category are – chimps, gorillas, orangutans and gibbons. Apes are bigger than the monkeys except the gibbons and have sharper intelligence. Apes do not have a tail but monkeys have a tail and use it has their fifth limb and to live a comfortable life on trees. Apes, however, have accustomed themselves to live on trees as well as on land. Also, monkeys cannot use their limbs to move from one tree to another, whereas apes have dexterity with limbs. The nasal opening of monkeys is slanted and that of apes is rounded.

23. Which is the most colourful monkey?

A Mandrill, found in the forests of Southern Cameroon, Gabon, Guinea and The Congo is the most colourful and also the largest monkey. A male Mandrill is more colourful than a female Mandrill and weighs roughly 50 kilograms, standing 3 feet tall. The coat of a Mandrill monkey is dark grey or olive green and is marked with bright, thick streaks of yellow and black. The face of a Mandrill monkey is hairless and is known for its peculiar, red muzzle, which is elongated and stretches down till its lips, which are red in colour, too. The muzzle has blue ridges on either side, adding more colours to a Mandrill's face. Its beard is yellow with tufts of white hair. The belly of a Mandrill is white in contrast to the colour of its coat and its lower body can be seen in a range of colours – red, pink, blue, scarlet and purple.

24. What is a bird?

Birds are unique members of the animal kingdom. With feathers and wings on their bodies and ability to lay eggs, birds are also warm-blooded. This means their body temperature remains the same under different weather conditions. You must know that there are scientists called ornithologists who study birds and their behaviour.

25. How do birds fly?

Birds have a light weight body as they have hollow bones. They also have strong wing muscles that help birds lift their light bodies for flight. The shape of the wings is called airfoil and it controls the air movement when they take a flight. The birds increase their speeds by flapping their wings and open their tails when they have to land on the ground or tree.

26. What are birds of prey?

Also known as raptors, birds of prey are those that eat meat and use their feet instead of beaks to capture their prey. Birds like vultures, falcons, eagles are gifted with sharp vision, strong beaks and feet muscles to hunt for their food.

27. Do all birds have the same kind of beaks?

The beaks or bills of birds differ from each other based on their eating, feeding, grooming and hunting habits. Birds of prey have short, stout and pointed beaks that help them tear the flesh of their prey. The humming bird has a long, slender beak that helps it to suck nectar from narrow flowers. Some birds have short and narrow beaks for catching small insects. The woodpecker has a slender, pointed beak for chipping off the tree barks. It is also interesting to note the long beak of the pelican acts as a fishing rod to catch fish in ponds.

28. Which bird's beak can hold more water than its stomach?

Pelicans are gifted with a long, slender beak and a large throat pouch. These birds use the throat pouches to catch fish. The moment the fish is trapped in the pouch, the pelicans move their heads forward and spill out the water. Pelicans are known to store about 11 litres of water not in their beaks but in their throat pouches, which is twice the amount they can store in their stomachs.

29. Which is the world's largest bird?

North African Ostrich is the world's largest bird. It can grow to 9 feet in height and weigh around 156 kilograms. These birds are valued for not only their feathers and meat, but also their skin that is made into the finest of leather. It is amazing to know that the ostrich has the largest eyes; each eye being up to 2 inches in diameter.

30. Which is the world's smallest bird?

The male Bee Hummingbird is the world's smallest bird; the females are slightly bigger. This bird weighs just about 1.8 grams and grows to a length of about 2 inches. This bird is so small that it is sometimes mistaken to be an insect. It can flap its wings at 80-beats-per-second. The eggs of this species are smaller than coffee beans!

31. Why do birds sit on their eggs?

We all know that birds lay eggs instead of giving birth to their young ones. The eggs are laid one at a time over a period of few hours or days. Once the eggs are laid, the mother bird ensures that the right temperature is maintained for the growth of the growing embryo. Too much cold or heat can harm the life growing inside the egg. Hence, birds sit on their eggs to give the right amount of heat. When the climate is very warm, birds even stand to give shade to their eggs, protecting them from the harsh Sun. Some birds like ducks even cover their eggs with feathers.

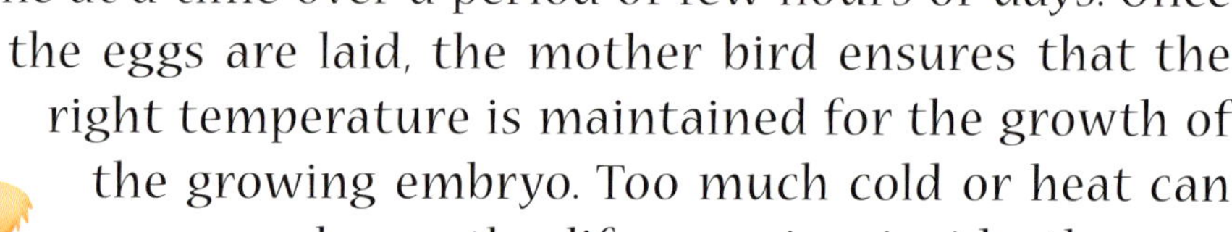

1. How do birds communicate?

Chirping of birds is like music to our ears. For the birds, it is their specialised way of communicating. Birds get their voice from an organ lying below their windpipe. This helps them sing songs or call out. A bird call is short and simple. It is inherited and taken out by both males and females. A bird song is longer and sung only by the males of some species. Bird songs are both inherited and learned from parents. Hence, different species of birds are identified by their unique sounds.

2. Which bird lays the biggest eggs?

The ostrich lays the biggest eggs. It is also the biggest bird that lives today, weighing as much as 130 kg. On an average, the egg is about 15 cm long, 13 cm wide, and weighs up to 1.4 kg, 30 times as much as a hen's egg. The egg shell is shiny, cream-coloured and pitted, and eggs are laid in a shallow pit dug by the bird. By day, the mother ostrich incubates the egg and the father ostrich warms the eggs by night.

3. Why do birds have feathers?

Feathers help birds to fly, to keep them warm and dry and protect them from predators as they can be effective camouflage. Scientists think that once some reptiles such as dinosaurs had feathers as insulation to keep them warm and dry. Over a long period of many billions of years, some of these reptiles started changing or evolving. They evolved feathers and wings and developed the ability to fly. Feathers are of different sizes and textures. An owl's feathers are soft and long, so it can fly quietly but slowly. A hawk's feathers are shorter and it flies faster. Birds that live on or near water have a coating of fine powder over their feathers, making them waterproof. All feathers fall out and are replaced when birds moult once a year.

4. Can all birds swim?

All birds are buoyant, which means that they have the ability to almost float on water. This is because they have hollow, air-filled bones. Those birds with webbed feet can swim better but all birds can swim or at least float on water. Some birds such as swans, ducks and geese, swim comfortably. Some birds such as cormorants and kingfishers dive into water to catch fish. Other birds such as penguins can swim under water and hold their breath for long periods of time.

5. Which is the fastest bird?

The fastest bird is the Peregrine Falcon, which can achieve a speed of over 200 miles per hour (mph). The Peregrine Falcon soars to a great height and then dives steeply to hunt its prey. However, it cannot sustain such a great speed when in level flight. In level flight, the fastest bird is the Spine-tailed Swift, which can travel at over 100 mph.

6. Why do birds migrate south in winter?

It has been observed that many species of birds make a regular seasonal journey every year. Birds may migrate to find food or because of changes in habitat or weather. Every year, certain birds migrate southwards before the onset of winter. Thus, they escape the harsh cold weather and move to warmer areas where they get sufficient food. In summer, they generally fly back to their original homes. The Arctic Tern has the longest migration route, as it migrates from its breeding grounds in the Arctic region, all the way to the Antarctic and back.

7. What are microorganisms?

Microorganisms are extremely small living beings, which are not visible to the naked eye. As their name suggests, they can only be seen by using a microscope. They are often single-celled organisms, like bacteria, viruses and fungi. Sometimes they are helpful to human beings. Some fungi, for example, help with fermentation, a process essential to make breads and cakes. Still other microorganisms, such as, certain viruses, are harmful to us, as they cause diseases in us and sometimes in our pets, too.

8. Which plant is really an animal?

The Sea Cucumbers look like plants but they are actually animals. Their shape and knobbly skin make them look a bit like a cucumber. But unlike cucumber plants, they can move around. Apart from these, there are certain plants that show the characteristics of animal life. For instance, there are plants such as the Venus Fly-trap and Pitcher Plant which trap insects and other small organisms for food. In fact, there are many creatures in the ocean which show features of both plants and animals!

9. Why do plants have roots?

The roots are the part of the plant that grow underneath the soil and firmly attach the plant in the soil so that it can grow upright. They also absorb water and other nutrients from their surroundings. These nutrients rise through the sap in the stem. In this way, the plant can feed and grow. As it grows taller, the roots get longer. Roots also act as food stores for plants. The roots are like the hearts of the plants, and without them, a plant will die.

10. Why do plants have leaves?

Leaves perform an important task for the plant by carrying water and processing plant food, so that it can grow properly. The stomata cells in the leaves separate the carbon dioxide from the oxygen with the help of sunlight, and combine this with other nutrients absorbed through the roots. This process is called photosynthesis. Leaves release the oxygen into the air. The lesser the sunlight, the larger the leaves will be in order to maximise surface area to capture the necessary amount of sunlight. For example, in the rainforests, the trees either grow tall or have really large leaves to be able to photosynthesise successfully. Food and water is also stored in leaves and these are rich in proteins, minerals and sugars. The outermost part of the leaf is the epidermis, the interior is the mesophyll that has the network of veins—xylem (transport water and minerals) and the phloem (transport dissolved sugar or sap).

11. Why do some leaves change colour in Autumn?

Leaf colour is determined by the amount of chlorophyll in them. In Autumn there is less sunlight and this makes the leaves produce less chlorophyll, and this is what changes the leaf colour. Chlorophyll is the green pigment produced as a product of photosynthesis. The rate at which the chlorophyll decays remains constant. Therefore, in cold conditions and when there is less sunlight, leaves will lose their green colour and turn red or brown, and dry up and even fall off.

12. Why do plants have stems?

The stem is an important part of the plant as it helps the plant to remain upright. The stems are rounded, tubular structures packed with dermal, ground and vascular tissues that perform different functions. The stem supports the growth of leaves, fruits and flowers, stores food for the plant and produces new cells. Water, nutrients and sap are carried around the plant by the stem. As plants grow, the stems grow taller and ensure that the leaves are high enough to absorb sunlight that is necessary for them to produce food and to live. As plants grow and depending on their type and size, some stems might become woody and hard over a period of time. There are different types of stems—bulbs (onion, tulip), vines (grapes), tuber (potato), corm (gladiolus), rhizomes (ferns, iris) and so on.

13. Why do trees lose their leaves?

Many trees lose their leaves in Winter because in the cold, the growth of trees slows down greatly. In the cold weather, less chlorophyll is produced, so the leaves turn brown, dry and die. Then, the tree has just enough water and nutrition stored in its trunk to stay alive till Spring arrives. The tree also rests during this time. In the cold Winter, in conditions of frost, the presence of leaves makes it difficult for them to survive. There are some tree species that retain their leaves throughout Winter. These are the evergreen trees, conifers such as pines, cedars and spruces, to name a few. These are used to the cold and have very deep roots that can reach water and nutrition, even in snowy conditions. When Spring arrives, temperatures go up and there is more sunlight, so new leaves grow and cover the tree once more.

14. Why do plants have flowers?

Flowers attract insects which help in pollination. Pollination is necessary for the survival of all plants, without which the species will die out. Pollination essentially means the transportation of pollen from one plant to another. The bright coloured flowers and their fragrance attracts insects. The insect such as a bee sucks the nectar and pollen from the flower stamens gets stuck to its body. Then the insect flies off to another plant with flowers. Here, the pollen that is stuck to its feet becomes deposited on the flower's stigma. This fertilises the plant and very soon, a fruit grows. The great variety of flowers and scents is nature's way to ensure that plant pollination and fertilisation will take place. Different types of insects pollinate different types of plants. For example, a particular type of butterfly will pollinate only one type of plant. Some plants are also capable of self-pollination.

15. How are seeds made?

When fertilisation occurs, the pollen deposited on the female flower, moves below the flower, into the topmost part of the stem, where there is a successful mixing of male and female DNA (the chemical building blocks of life) and it ripens. The ripened portion/fruit develops soon after. This contains one or many seeds. A seed has an embryo, a supply of food and an outer covering. There are seeds that have a hard outer covering ('stone' fruits such as the peach), while others have a soft covering such as the bean.

16. How do seeds grow?

The process by which the seeds grow is called germination. From one end of the seed, a little shoot emerges when the seed gets as much soil, sunlight and water as it needs. This first shoot is called a radicle, which burrows into the soil to find nutrition. This radicle develops into the main or tap root, from which root branches will grow. When the radicle has grown strong enough, the stem or plumule grows upwards, out of the soil. This grows up to a certain height and the leaves start forming. Seeds may be intentionally or accidentally planted. Many plants are grown for their seeds, which are then planted and harvested—wheat, rice, and vegetables that you eat are grown this way. Seeds sticking to animal and insect bodies are spread naturally, when it comes off their bodies and falls into soil.

17. What do seeds need to grow?

Seeds need carbon dioxide, minerals, water and sunlight to grow. When there is enough moisture and sunlight, the seed swells and the seed coat bursts open to allow the seed to grow. Overwatering, excessively dry conditions, harsh temperatures, planting the seed too deeply, and improper conditions like these can cause the germination process to fail. Use of strong pesticides and chemicals over a long duration is also likely to result in failed germination.

18. Which seeds can fly?

Many seeds are small in size and light in weight and can be easily picked up and carried along in the air by a breeze. Seeds from trees such as Hornbeam, Sycamore, Ash and smaller plants such as Puya, Dandelion, Milkweed and so on, are dispersed by the wind. Some seeds have stiff wings covering them, while some wings are twisted, making it easier for them to be picked up by even a slight breeze. Some seeds have fine hair-like filaments and are also easily carried by the wind. Orchid seeds are very fine, so they are blown as easily as dust. In this way, they cover long distances.

19. What is the timber line?

The timber line or tree line is the last extent till which trees can grow. Generally, beyond the timber line, the weather conditions are too cold or dry for trees to grow. Trees near the edge of the timber line are usually smaller and stunted. Seen from a distance, the edge of the timber line seems to have a dense canopy, beyond which trees abruptly stop growing. This phenomenon is seen in both cold mountainous and desert environments.

20. Which plants live in sea water?

There are many plants that grow in sea water, most commonly, the sea grasses of various kinds. These deep sea plants are rooted in the sandy sea beds. They bear flowers and cover wide expanses, almost like a meadow. They complete their entire lifecycle under water. The turtle grass is one such type of sea grass. Its plants have long, narrow leaves and are green. Since they need sunlight to photosynthesise, this grass grows in the lighted or photic sea zones, around the shallow and protected coastal waters, in sandy, muddy soils. For example, in Chesapeake Bay, there are more than 16 species of underwater or submerged aquatic vegetation growing. These provide a home to various animals such as fish, shellfish and waterfowl. These add oxygen to the air, trap soil, slow down the wave action and protect the shoreline from being eroded.

21. Are some plants dangerous?

Yes, some plants are definitely dangerous. Some are poisonous to touch, such as Milkweeds and Poison Oak. Some can cause mild to severe health problems when eaten or breathed. For example, windblown pollen can cause allergies or Hay Fever. Toxalbumins are plant poisons that can cause death to mammals, like Ragwort, Hogs Weed, Poison Ivy, Wild Black Cherry, Azalea, Castor Bean, Rosary Pea, Monkshood, Bushman's Poison, Sngel's Trumpet, Hemlock and Bittersweet. Borage and Calamus cause skin irritation and stomach upsets. Some of these poisonous plants have also been used for medicinal purposes when properly processed and consumed in the correct quantities. Valerian is one such medicine.

22. Which plants have weapons?

Plants that are carnivorous or insectivorous have developed different defence mechanisms that keep them safe from predators. It is also nature's way to ensure that they get a steady supply of food. There are about 630 species of such plants. As these plants usually grow on nitrogen-deficient soil, they need to consume insects and other animals for their nitrogen supply. Most of these are highly colourful and have sac-like structures or highly sticky surfaces that trap prey. Pitfall traps in pitcher plants trap prey in a rolled leaf that contains a pool of digestive enzymes or bacteria. Flypaper traps use a sticky mucilage along a long tentacle, from which an insect cannot escape. Plants with snap traps quickly shut their leaves around their victims, while bladder traps literally suck their prey into an interior vacuum. The poky hair on either side of a lobster-pot trap forces its prey to keep moving until it reaches the digestive organ.

23. Which plants can we eat?

The non-poisonous plants that have seeds and fruits can be eaten. Over a period of time, man has experimented and cultivated those plants which are nutritious and can be easily grown. A variety of grains, such as wheat, rice, millets and corn (plant seeds), provide the basic carbohydrates, some minerals and sugar you need to survive. Apart from this, cultivated food plants such as the vegetables (beans, tomatoes, cauliflowers, gourds, squashes, and so on) and roots (onions, ginger, turmeric, potatoes, yams, carrots) are edible and provide many of the minerals and vitamins you need. Most of the fruits are edible—mangoes, apples, peaches, plums, grapes and bananas are eatable and highly nutritious. Herbs of various kinds, like thyme, chives, coriander, sage and others are added to food as spices and are healthy for you. Tea and coffee also come from plants—tea is a dried leaf, and coffee comes from dried and roasted beans. Soya milk is made from the white soya bean.

24. Can I help to protect plants?

Yes, you must do what you can to protect and grow plants. Since there are so many useful plants, depending on how much land/space you have, you can grow selected plants in your own home. There are many plants that are going to die out as species because of over-use or shifting its location. It is important to follow good gardening practices—if you see an attractive plant in the wild, leave it there. Moving it from its natural location will probably be harmful for the plant. There are organisations that protect natural habitats. You can always volunteer and work with them or donate money so that they can carry on their work. Be more aware of what is happening to the natural environment around you, use less paper (it is made of tree pulp), plant new trees and grow beautiful gardens. In this way, you will have a patch of nature in your own home.

25. How do plants help us?

Plants help us in many ways. The most important factor is that plants take in carbon dioxide from the air and release oxygen, which we need to survive. Thus, plants give us the air we breathe in. Plants also provide us with food that we eat as fruits, vegetables, roots and shoots. Therefore, they are an important source of our nutrition, too. In addition, plants play an important role in controlling the weather and climatic conditions in any part of the Earth.

26. Do apples, onions and potatoes taste the same?

Apples, onions and potatoes are objectively very different in their tastes. However, if you happen to taste these three food items with your nose plugged, you will find them of the same taste. In other words, you will not be able to tell the difference in the taste of these foods. This shows that it is not only the taste buds on our tongues but also our nose that plays a role in our sense of taste. There are specialised smell cells in the upper reaches of our nose. Chewing food sends chemicals to these special nose cells and they send signals to our brain.

27. Are apple seeds poisonous?

It has been found that eating apple pits or seeds in bulk can cause food poisoning. Excessive dosage can be dangerous as apple seeds have the toxin cyanogenic glycoside or cyanide in them. Although swallowing the seeds of a single apple is generally harmless for an adult, children should be more careful.

28. What do our eyebrows do?

Our evolutionary ancestors had hair all over their faces. With time, hair on our face became sparse, but the eyebrows were retained. Eyebrows must have served certain purposes like protecting the eyes from dust, rain and sweat. Eyebrows also play a very interesting role in face recognition, conveying emotions and non-verbal communication.

29. Why is juggling good for our brain?

We clearly understand that our brain is the seat of all intellectual activity. Scientists have been able to show that by engaging in certain activities, we can stimulate the nerve cells that make up our brain and in turn make our brains function better for a longer period of time. Scientists carried out a study where they involved people in the activity of juggling over a period of some months. Brain scans of these people showed increased levels of activity in the brain.

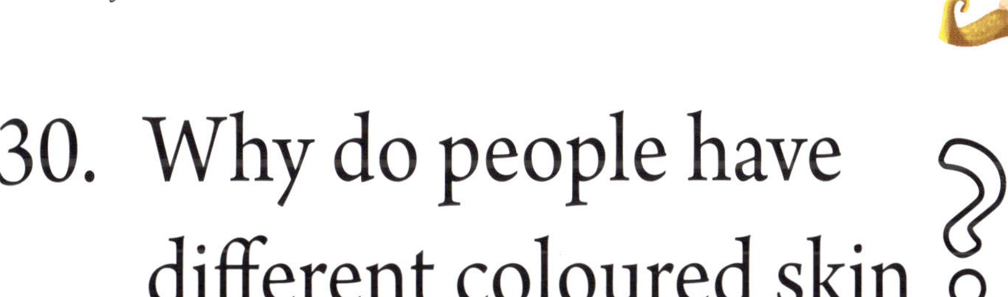

30. Why do people have different coloured skin?

People around the world have different coloured skin. This is not due to any social, religious or cultural reasons. The difference in the skin colour is due to the presence of a pigment called Melanin.

People with darker colour tones have more of this pigment while people with lighter skin tone have less of this pigment. This pigment is activated when the skin is exposed to the Sun. Hence, over a period of time, people staying in hot, sunny regions developed more of melanin and became dark-skinned, while people living in areas with less sunrays, remained light-skinned.

1. Where does food go after we swallow it?

When we swallow, the food goes into a tube called the oesophagus or the food pipe. The oesophagus is a muscular tube that is connected to the stomach. The muscles that surround the oesophagus help to squeeze and push the food into the stomach.

2. How long does it take for the food to get digested?

Digestion means breaking down of food into smaller forms, releasing the nutrients and energy that our bodies can use. Food is considered to be completely digested when the nutrients are retained and the waste is expelled from our bodies. The time taken for this process varies in terms of the nature of food eaten, individual bodies and other conditions like medical disorder and stress. On an average, it takes 24-72 hours for food to be completely digested.

3. What are we made of?

Do you know that our bodies are mostly made up of water? This is something that we humans and our planet Earth have in common! Roughly 60 per cent of our weight is actually composed of water. Another 20 per cent of our weight is fat. The remaining 20 per cent is constituted by protein, carbohydrates, vitamins, minerals and some natural biochemicals.

4. Is our spine important for our body to function?

Our spine or backbone is a strong, flexible column of ring-like bones that runs from our skull to our pelvis. It is because of our backbone that we are able to hold our head and body upright. We can also bend and twist our bodies. The spine protects our spinal cord, which is a large bundle of nerves running through the cavity in the centre of your spine. These nerves connect our body functions with our brain, helping us to function properly.

5. What do our kidneys do?

We have a pair of kidneys that help our bodies clean our bloodstream and maintain the chemical balance in our bodies. When the process of digestion is complete and nutrients are extracted, the waste mixes in the bloodstream. The kidneys filter the blood and the resulting wastes and extra water become urine, which flows to the bladder. The bladder stores urine until released through urination.

6. What are hair and nails made of and what function do they serve?

Our hair and our nails both are made out of the same material called keratin. Interestingly, both these parts do not have nerves in them; hence we do not feel anything when the extended nails or hair are trimmed. The living part of hair is the part in the scalp and for the nails, in the skin. Nails provide support for the tips of the fingers and toes and protect them from injury. The hair on our bodies keep the heat away.

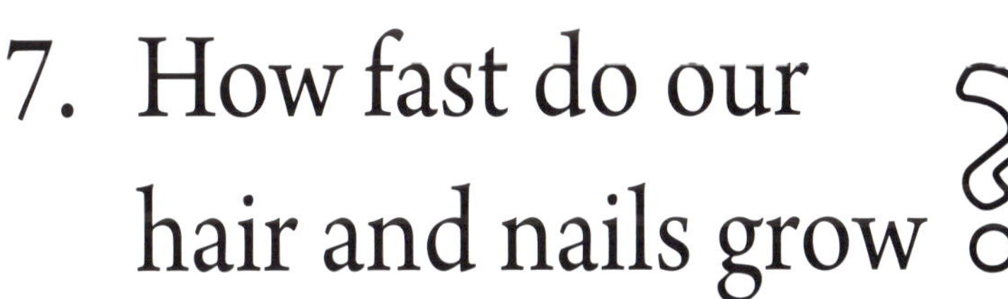

7. How fast do our hair and nails grow?

The rate at which our hair and nail grow varies from person to person. Generally, hair grows at an average of half an inch or 1.25 centimetres per month. Due to the cold in Winter, hair grows slowly, whereas, in Spring and Summer, it grows a little faster. Nails grow far more quickly than hair. They grow at an average rate of one-eighth of an inch or 3 millimetres every month.

8. Why does it not hurt when we cut our hair and nails?

Trimming nails and getting a haircut is a painless process. The parts of our hair and nails that lie above the skin's surface are made up of keratin. Keratin is comprised of dead cells of a tough protein. Since these cells are dead, there is no sensitivity. Thus, when we cut our hair or nails, there is no sensation whatsoever. However, nails and hair have nerve endings just below the skin's surface. If our hair is pulled or we cut our nails too short, these nerves are affected and this could hurt us.

9. What are hiccups?

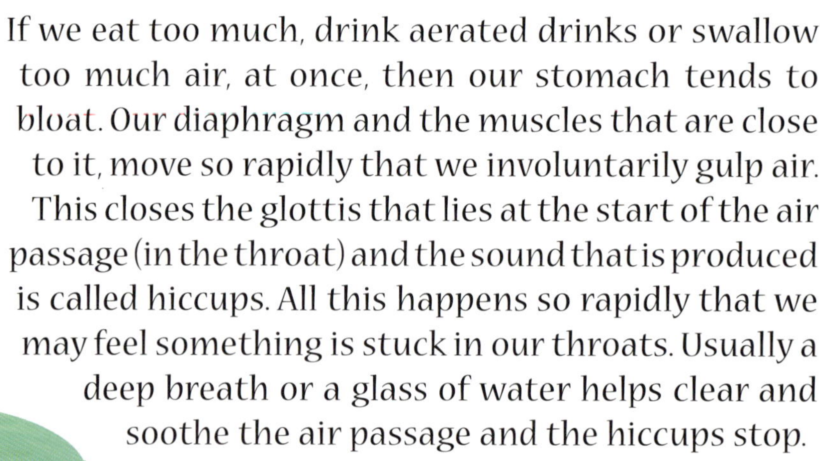

If we eat too much, drink aerated drinks or swallow too much air, at once, then our stomach tends to bloat. Our diaphragm and the muscles that are close to it, move so rapidly that we involuntarily gulp air. This closes the glottis that lies at the start of the air passage (in the throat) and the sound that is produced is called hiccups. All this happens so rapidly that we may feel something is stuck in our throats. Usually a deep breath or a glass of water helps clear and soothe the air passage and the hiccups stop.

10. Why do we need to breathe?

We need to breathe to live, as without breathing, human life cannot survive. We need oxygen that is present in the air to breathe as it imparts energy to the body and mind so that they can function properly. If we breathe properly, we think more clearly, digest our food better, have good muscular and nerve co-ordination and good energy levels so that we do everything else well. When we breathe out, we expel carbon-dioxide (a waste product) from our bodies. When going underwater, humans breathe through a special mouthpiece connected to an oxygen cylinder strapped on their backs.

11. How do we breathe in and out?

We breathe through our nose and lungs that comprise the respiratory system. The chest and abdomen expands and contracts as we breathe in and out. Both the ribs and the abdominal area rise and increase the surface area of air taken in. This is called costal (ribs) and abdominal (lower body) breathing, and both occur simultaneously. Air is drawn in through the nostrils and it passes into the lungs. The air then passes into the blood stream circulating in the body. From here, the cells absorb the necessary oxygen. The blood circulates back to the lungs and the air absorbs the waste products. As we breathe out, we release this air. In this process, the lungs act as a pair of bellows, deflating and inflating and controlling the intake of air. The lungs rest on the diaphragm and this is the main muscle responsible for breathing.

12. How fast do we breathe?

Breathing is a continuous process. We already have air in our lungs when the blood passes through for getting fresh oxygen and releasing carbon-dioxide. If there is already enough oxygen in the blood, then it will absorb less oxygen. If we are sleeping, the body is at rest and needs a minimum of oxygen, so we breathe slowly. On the other hand, when we are running or climbing, we burn energy faster, so we need more oxygen. We will also need to get rid of the greater amount of carbon-dioxide that has accumulated. So, we will breathe out faster. Thus, the rate at which we breathe depends upon the activity we are doing.

13. Why do we sneeze?

The nose is an extremely sensitive organ that regulates the air we breathe. So, it makes sure we breathe clean, healthy air. Air sometimes has tiny particles that are unsuitable for us. When we sneeze, our nostrils expel the irritating particles. It could be dust, pollen, various food smells, among other things. People with allergies can react to a variety of substances like paints, foods and even perfumes, and they often sneeze a lot. When we have bad colds and stuffy noses, we sneeze. In this way, our body removes harmful substances that have gathered inside.

14. How do our lungs work?

The lungs (the right and left lung) are located in the upper part of the body, within the thoracic or chest cavity. These help us to breathe. These are large, highly elastic organs whose function is to provide a space where oxygen can reach the blood and carbon-dioxide can be removed. The lungs have to be connected to the outside to work—the nose provides the passage for air intake. The nose is connected to the lungs through a windpipe (trachea). This sends air directly to the lungs. The windpipe divides into two main vessels (left and right bronchus) and these subdivide further inside the lungs. The lungs have thin membranes (pleura) on their surface covering highly spongy, elastic tissue with air and blood vessels. The tiniest balloon-like air sacs are called alveoli. The tiniest blood vessels (pulmonary capillaries) are wrapped around each alveolus. The exchange of oxygen and carbon-dioxide occurs between the alveoli and capillaries. With each breath, our air supply is regulated—when we breathe in, we take in oxygen and when we breathe out, carbon-dioxide is released.

15. How do we see?

We see through our eyes, located in bony sockets, just below our foreheads. When we look at something what we are actually 'seeing' is the light that is reflected off the object's surface. The eye is a ball-shaped organ. The outermost part is the cornea and when we close our eyes, the eyelids cover it. There is a thin tissue that runs behind the eye, which is the white part of the eye and is called the sclera. The ciliary muscles lie at the front ends of the sclera. The retina is a membrane composed of rod and cone receptor cells, and lies in the back of the eyes, over the sclera. It is light-sensitive and transmits light to the nerves. Between the retina and cornea, the rounded eye is filled with aqueous humour, a watery substance. In the front and centre of the retina is the pupil. Light passes through the cornea and the pupil to the retina. From here, nerve muscles are activated by the light and travel through the optic nerve to our brains (the occipital lobe just above the back of the neck). Then our brains send back information as to what we are looking at. Both eyes work together and this is called binocular vision.

16. Why do we shed tears?

The eyes have tear glands at the outer corner of the eye behind the upper eyelid. These are about the size of almonds. These are called the lachrymal glands. When we blink, these glands release a salty solution that washes the eyes. This liquid passes over the eyes and drains into the tear duct in the inner corner of the eye. Sometimes, due to various reasons (happiness, sadness) there is excessive blood flow to the face or increased pressure in the head. This causes the upper eyelid muscles to squeeze the lacrimal gland. This causes an excessive build up of tears in the glands and tears spill over the eye's surface and we shed tears.

17. Why do our pupils change size?

Around the pupil is a coloured band of muscle called the iris. Depending upon the amount of light required for our eyes to see, the pupil will need to take in more or less light. So, the iris will contract and expand to make the pupil smaller or bigger. If we are close to an object, our pupils will contract, as less light is required. Likewise, in the dark or while reading fine print, better focusing is required, so the pupil will expand to allow more light inside. This happens automatically; the brighter the light, the quicker the pupils will contract and vice versa. If not, then excessive or dim light can damage the retinal cells. If we step out from a dark room into the sunlight, it takes a few seconds for us to see properly. This is because the pupil is readjusting its size as per the light. When we watch anything that is going by very quickly or we are travelling very fast, our vision may get blurred as the rate of expansion and contraction of the pupil is too rapid to allow a steady image.

18. Why are people's eyes of different colours?

The iris is the coloured part of the eye. The colour is inherited and does not affect vision in any way. People from different parts of the world tend to have a similar range of eye colours. The colour of the iris will also depend upon genetic, family traits. If our parents have brown eyes, we will most probably have brown eyes, too. The colour of the iris varies from shades of blue to brown to black to even green.

19. Do carrots help us see in the dark?

Carrots contain a high amount of beta-carotene. If we eat carrots, the body converts this into Vitamin A, which is essential to maintain healthy eyesight. If there is less Vitamin A in our bodies, we may start having eye problems. We will not be able to see clearly in dim light. Basically, retinal rods contain a colour, visual purple. The amount of this colour depends upon the amount of Vitamin A in the body. So, if we do not have enough Vitamin A, we may develop night blindness. The eye can only see if it recreates this colour in the retina in dim and dark conditions. So, eating carrots and other sources of Vitamin A is good for our eyes.

20. What is colour blindness?

The retinal cones are responsible for distinguishing between various colours. Due to genetic factors, disease, eye, nerve or brain damage, many people lose this ability and become colour blind. Mainly, they are unable to differentiate between red and green. In extreme cases of colour blindness, everything appears in shades of grey.

21. How do we smell?

The nose is the organ responsible for smelling in our body. When we breathe in, we also sense the different smells in the air. The nose is mainly made of cartilage and bone and covered with a thin layer of skin outside. There are two internal divisions—the nostrils and the central part is the septum. Air is warmed and moistened in the nostrils. The olfactory nerves, located in the top part of the nose, actually detect smells. The odours pass through as tiny particles or even molecules of gas across the nerve endings that pass through the nasopharynx (at the top of the throat) and into the lower part of the brain. The brain cells identify the smell and enable us to distinguish between them. What is interesting is that only inhaled air can be smelt while exhaled air passes straight out.

22. What is our tongue for?

The tongue is a muscle that helps us taste, chew and swallow food. It also helps us to talk clearly. It is, therefore, an important muscle. It lies on the floor of the mouth, and is attached to the back of the throat and mouth with other muscles. A mucous membrane called mucosa covers the tongue and reacts to change in temperature and texture. It has various kinds of projections called papillae that contain the taste buds. These taste buds are sense organs that send nerve impulses to the brain. Once the tongue has mixed the food with saliva and it is well chewed, the food is sent into the digestive tract. The tongue contracts and pushes the food through the food pipe or oesophagus and it travels further down. The tongue also helps us speak. By touching or not touching the roof of the mouth and the teeth, sounds are formed. A healthy tongue is pink and moist, with a velvety look. Only animals with backbones have true tongues.

23. How strong is our sense of smell?

The sense of smell in humans is not as well developed as that of other animals, but it is acute. Many different types of smells—from light fragrances to bad odours—are recognisable by humans. It takes a few seconds to know what is being smelled. The strength of the smell depends on distance, quantity and the nature of the smell itself. Rotting garbage can be smelled from far away. To smell a perfume, one has come close to the flower or the person wearing it. When we have bad colds, we cannot smell anything because all our olfactory nerves are closed. The health of the nose and olfactory nerves determine how well humans can smell.

24. What makes our mouths smell?

If there is any smelly substance on our tongues or teeth, our mouths will smell. This could be a bad or good smell. People who have clean teeth and good digestions have no particular mouth smell. On the other hand, if we have poor digestion or kidney and liver disorders, diabetes or other medical problems then gas could come back up the food pipe and be breathed out. Our mouths will have sour, sweet or foul smells and we will suffer from unpleasant breath. Bad breath is also called halitosis. If we do not clean our teeth properly, tooth infection may set in and cause bad breath. If our tongues have yellowish, whitish or other coloured coatings, then our mouths are bound to have some unhealthy smell. A proper diet, exercise and dental hygiene will take care of unpleasant mouth smells.

25. Why do people get wrinkles when they grow older?

The skin is the most important organ in our body. It consists of two layers: the upper layer called epidermis and the lower layer called dermis. The outer layer dries up, flakes off and is renewed from the layer below. The dermis (layer of living cells) works to make the tough protein layer that will eventually become part of the epidermis. The epidermis also contains elastic fibres that help the skin retain its elasticity. Sebaceous glands in the dermis secrete semi-oily fluid that lubricates the skin and hair. As we grow, the sebaceous glands secrete less fluid and this affects the elasticity of the dermis. As the moisture in the epidermis decreases, the skin dries up faster and becomes looser. This dried, loose skin develops furrows. These tiny furrows are wrinkles.

26. Why do we sweat?

By sweating, the body regulates body temperature. When the body gets heated, then we sweat and release moisture in the form of tiny droplets of water that cools the body as it evaporates. We also sweat to release substances that our body does not require. The eccrine glands are under the arms and produce a fluid that comes out of the skin pores, creating wetness. There are apocrine glands over the rest of our skin that release secretions. These are broken down by bacteria on the skin surface.

Our body usually gets rid of waste material through urine and excreta, and through the nose (in case of a bad cold). Sometimes, when this is not enough, the waste material is released through sweat. Sweat can also smell strongly depending on our diet and state of health. The maximum number of sweat glands is found in the palms and soles—almost 3,000 to the square inch, six times as much when compared to the rest of the body.

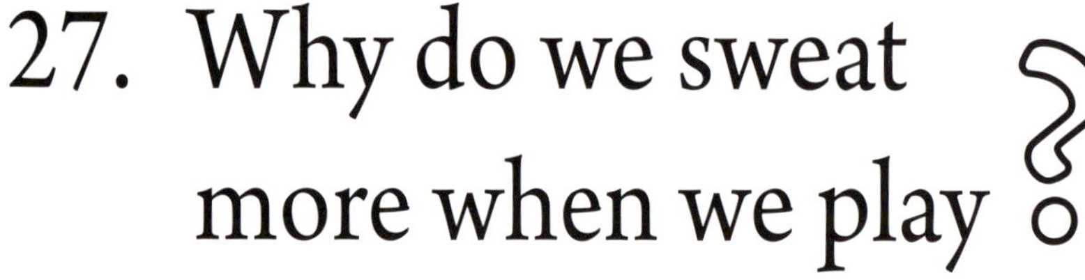

27. Why do we sweat more when we play?

Sweat helps to cool the body off during play or exercise. One must watch out for the level of sweating. If our body is covered in a fine film of moisture, it's perfectly healthy. However, reaching a state where sweat is dripping, shows the body is sttruggling to cool down and is overworked. One must drink plenty of fluids to make up for water lost by sweating.

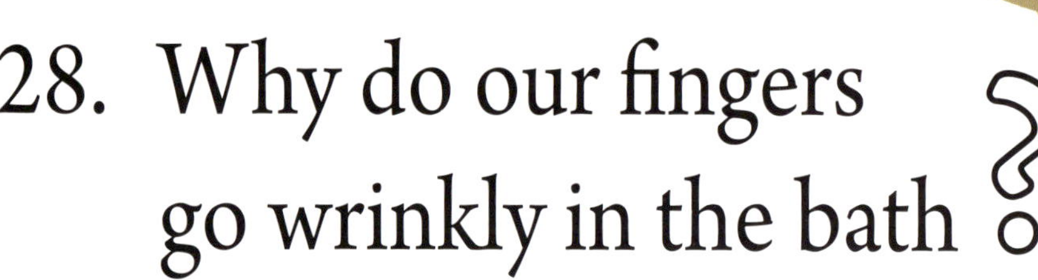

28. Why do our fingers go wrinkly in the bath?

Under normal circumstances, our bodies are covered in essential natural oil. This natural oil protects our skin from foreign substances. However, when we are in a tub, a pool or the shower for a long time, this natural oil is washed away by the water. Now, the water is free to enter through the skin and make it water-logged. It is because of this water-logging that our fingers go wrinkly. The rest of our body has a thicker coat of natural oil, so the water does not wash it away entirely.

29. Why do we get goose bumps?

The hair on our skin is held in place by the Pili Muscle. It is located at the end of our body hairs, where it is rooted in the skin. Now, when we are feeling cold or frightened, the Pili Muscles contract. This makes our body hair stand on the end. Hence, we get goose bumps or gooseflesh. Scientists and doctors, however, call it *Piloerection,* meaning erection of hair due to activity in the Pili Muscle.

30. Why do some people have straight hair and some curly?

The kind of hair that a person has is dependent on his or her genetic structure. The shaft of our hair contains proteins. These proteins, in turn, carry chemical bonds known as disulfide bonds. Now, if a person has a large number of disulfide bonds in the hair shaft, he or she will have curly hair. On the other hand, if disulfide bonds are fewer in number, a person's hair will be straight. Hence, straight or curly hair is entirely dependent on a person's genes.

31. Where is our Funny Bone?

Our Funny Bone is located at our elbow. Actually, the 'Funny Bone' is not really a bone, but a nerve! This nerve is called the Ulnar Nerve and it runs on the inside of our elbow. When we bump our elbow in the area of this nerve, it causes a tingling sensation that runs to our last two fingers. It is a funny feeling, which is why the area came to be known as the Funny Bone.

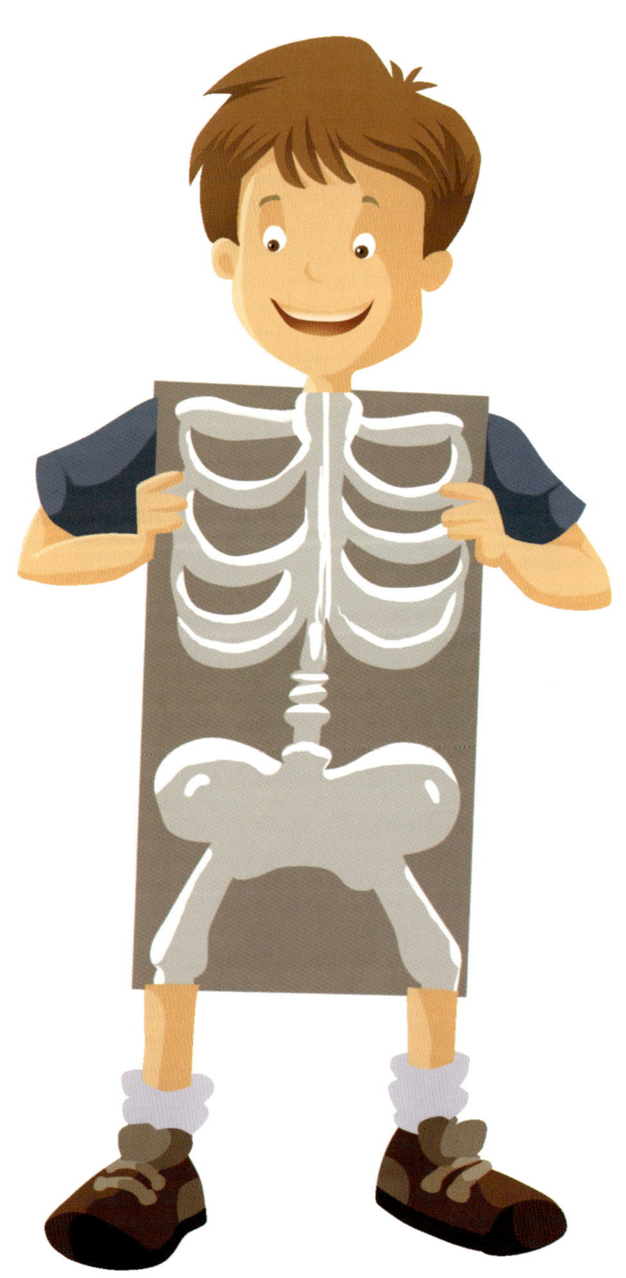

1. What do muscles do?

The basic and foremost function of muscles is to cause locomotion or movement. All our movement in the body takes place because of the presence of muscles. It may be simple and voluntary movement, such as, lifting our arm, walking and running or an involuntary movement, such as, the pumping of our heart, the working of the digestive system, and so on. Either way, muscles provide force and motion to the body and internal organs.

2. How do different muscles work?

There are different types of muscles: skeletal, voluntary and involuntary. Of these, skeletal muscles expand and contract with the help of units called sarcomeres. Voluntary and involuntary muscles, on the other hand, are controlled by the brain. Our brain uses nerve signals that order the muscle to contract and cause movement.

3. Where does our food go after we eat it?

After we swallow our food, it goes through a complex digestive process in our body. A tube called the oesophagus runs down our throat and transmits the chewed food down to our stomach. Our stomach then acts like a mixing sack, where certain chemicals, called digestive juices, mix with the food and finely grind it. This ground and mixed food is then released into the small intestine, where it is converted into carbohydrates, proteins and fats. Once this is done, the carbohydrates and proteins are released into our bloodstream, so that our body can use them for energy. The fats are released into the lymph system. Of the remaining matter, water is absorbed by the large intestine and solids are pushed out of the body through the anus.

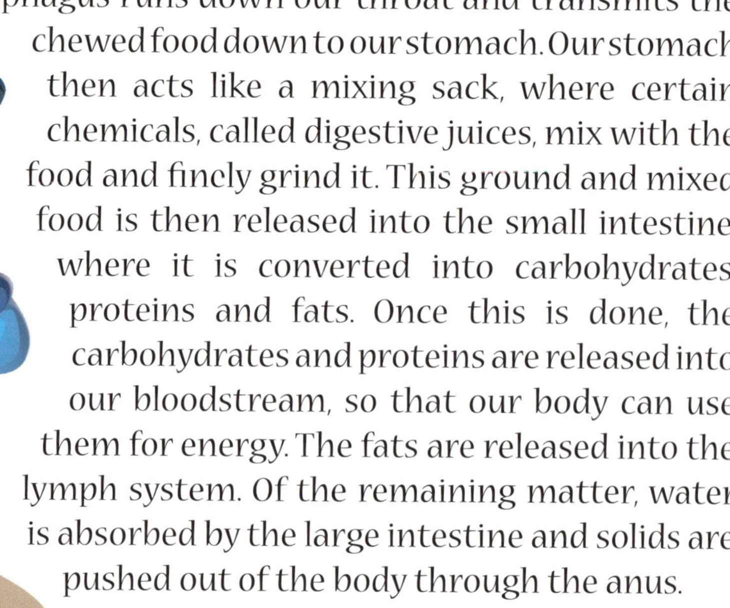

4. What are teeth for?

We know that teeth help us chew and grind our food. There are four types of teeth—incisors, canines, molars and pre-molars. Incisors help us bite into our food. Canines are sharp and pointed, so they help us tear the food. Next, the pre-molars help us grind the food. Finally, molars help us chew the ground food. However, the teeth are not just for eating food. As jaws, they provide a structure to our facial muscles. It is because of this that we are able to form certain expressions, like a frown. In fact, when we smile, it shows on the lips, with the help of jaws! Our teeth also work with our tongue movements when we speak to help us make sounds.

5. What is the function of blood?

The main function of blood is to act as a carrier for oxygen, from the lungs to the various body tissues. Oxygen, as we know, is vital for living. It also takes care of the nutrients, hormones and enzymes from our metabolism. Further, it controls our body temperature, water content, acid-base balance and blood clotting. Blood contains antibodies and white cells too, which protect us from parasites and diseases.

6. What work does our heart do?

Our heart is made up of muscles and is a little larger than our fist. It is actually a pump that generates healthy blood that is rich in oxygen, to be sent to the rest of the body. Blood flows from all parts of the body to the heart, through the veins. This blood is devoid of oxygen. The heart pumps oxygen into it. This oxygen-rich blood then travels to the rest of our body through arteries. The beat that we hear and feel is actually the sound of our pumping heart. It beats around 100,000 times each day!

7. Where is our heart located?

Our heart is located in the inside of our chest, to our left. Internally, it lies behind the lungs and above our diaphragm. It contains four chambers: the upper chambers are called right and left atrium and the lower chambers are called right and left ventricle, respectively.

8. Can we feel our heart beating?

Yes, we can feel our heart beating. Under normal conditions, we can place a hand on the left side of our chest and feel the beats. We can also put our ear to another person's chest and hear their heart beats. We can especially hear and feel our heart when we exercise, or feel nervous or scared. Our heart beats much faster, then. Thus, we can feel it more easily.

9. What happens when we breathe?

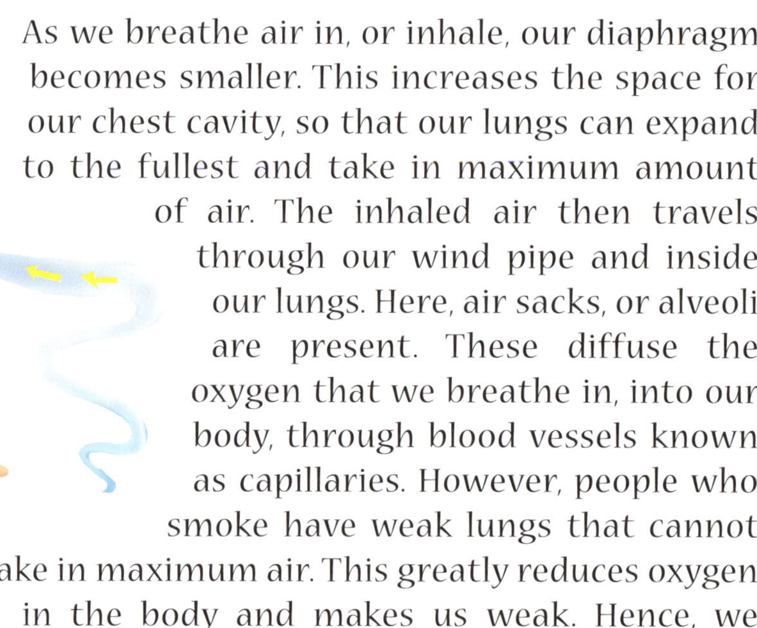

As we breathe air in, or inhale, our diaphragm becomes smaller. This increases the space for our chest cavity, so that our lungs can expand to the fullest and take in maximum amount of air. The inhaled air then travels through our wind pipe and inside our lungs. Here, air sacks, or alveoli are present. These diffuse the oxygen that we breathe in, into our body, through blood vessels known as capillaries. However, people who smoke have weak lungs that cannot take in maximum air. This greatly reduces oxygen in the body and makes us weak. Hence, we should never smoke.

10. What makes us yawn?

Yawning occurs mainly because of tiredness. In fact, even when we are bored, we breathe in slower than usual. Thus, our body is not getting as much oxygen as it usually does. So, in order to release extra carbon dioxide, yawning occurs. It is actually a huge gulp of air, as the body attempts to make up for the slow intake of oxygen.

11. What do pancreas do?

The pancreas is actually a set of glands that function as an organ. This organ is located in the abdomen, where it secretes various enzymes and other chemicals. These help in the digestive process by breaking down food into smaller units, such as, carbohydrates and proteins. These smaller units are in the form in which our bodies can use them. Hence, the pancreas perform an important function that helps us remain energised.

12. What does our brain do?

The brain is an extremely important organ of our body. It is the central commander of our entire nervous system. Not only this, it is also where our memory is stored. Also, all our emotions, behaviour, thoughts originate from our brain. Apart from this, the brain also controls physical phenomena in our body, such as, blood pressure, heartbeat, movement, posture and other internal activity.

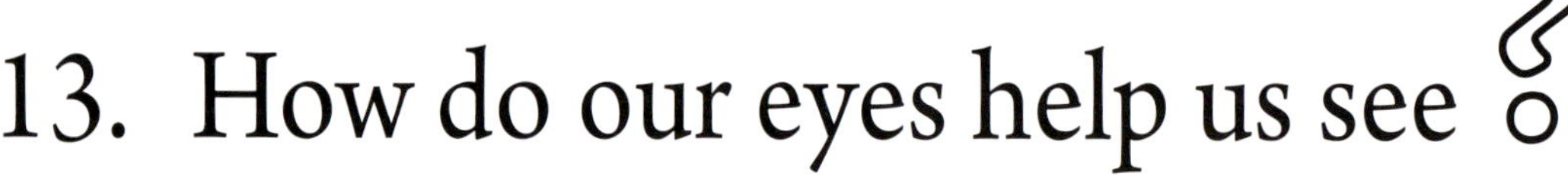

13. How do our eyes help us see?

Our eyes coordinate with the brain to help us see. The light rays from various objects that surround us, enter our eye through the cornea. These light rays then pass through the lens of our eye, which focuses them. The focused light then forms an image on the retina, which is a screen-like mechanism at the back of our eye. This image is actually upside down! The brain then converts this into signals that make up our sense of sight. This is how we perceive, or see, our surroundings.

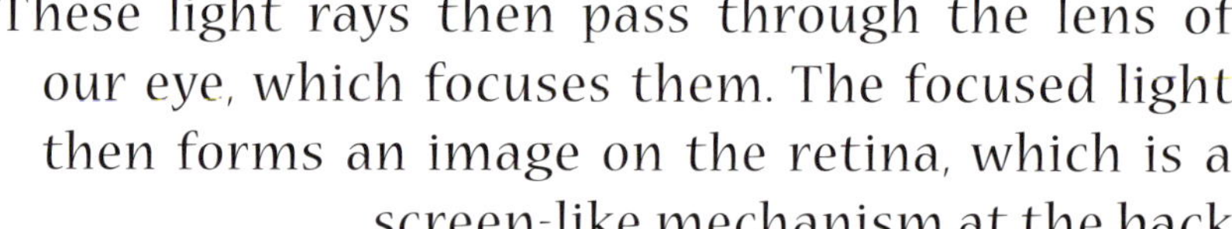

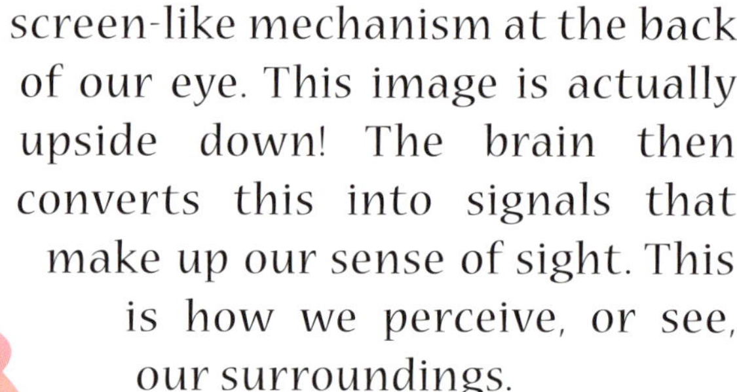

14. How do our ears help us hear?

Each of our ears is made up of three sections: the outer ear, middle ear and the inner ear. Sound waves are collected in the outer ear, also known as the ear canal. Then these waves are streamed into the inside of the ear, where they hit the eardrum. This produces vibration in the process, which takes place in the middle ear. The middle ear amplifies these vibrations and sends them further on into the inner ear. Here, the vibrations convert into a wave. This wave then travels through the hearing nerve. Then, it reaches the brain through the acoustic nerve, in the form of electro-chemical signals. Thus, sound waves are converted into the sensation of hearing.

15. What is our nose for?

The nose serves us through many functions. First, it helps us breathe. There are small hair-like structures inside our nostrils that filter the air that we inhale. The nose also helps to warm and moisten the inhaled air, so that when it reaches the lungs, it is not harmful. This is why we are advised to avoid breathing through our mouth, since it performs no such protective functions. Another function of the nose, as we all know, is the sense of smell. It tells us whether our food is rotten or safe to eat, or the place that we are going to is clean or dirty and smelly!

16. Why can we not taste food when we have a cold?

Did you know that our nose and our tongue work together, especially when we are dealing with food? The nose helps us smell the food and the tongue helps us taste it, through its taste buds. This is how we can recognise, taste and appreciate the various flavours of food and drink. However, when we have a cold, our nose and its upper pores are clogged. So, the nose is putting most of its effort to help us breathe in properly. Thus, our sense of smell and taste are both weakened. We are prone to absorb more salt than any other flavour, so that all food that we taste seems bland and tasteless!

17. What is chickenpox?

Chickenpox is a disease that is caused by microorganisms. These viral microorganisms are known as the *Varicella Zoster* virus. They cause blister-like eruptions all over our skin, which are very itchy. Chickenpox is also a contagious disease. This means that it can spread when a person affected by it comes in physical or close contact with other people. Apart from the characteristic itchy blisters, chickenpox also causes fever, low appetite and tiredness.

18. Why do we get sick sometimes?

In our everyday routine, as we go to school, to our backyard, play with our friends, or even roam around indoors, we come in contact with many kinds of virus and bacteria. These are extremely small creatures and cannot be seen through the naked eye. However, many of these are harmful to the body. Although our immunity system fights many of these harmful organisms, sometimes there are too many of them for our body to deal with. This is when we fall sick. Apart from this, there are other reasons like unhealthy food, impure water, certain mosquitoes and so on, that make us fall ill.

19. What is our belly button?

Every person has a belly button. It is also known as the navel. It is located in the centre of our belly. This is the place where, as an embryo inside our mother's stomach, we were attached to her through a cord. This cord is called the umbilical cord and is cut off at the time of birth. Did you know that like fingerprints each person has a unique belly button!

20. Why do we sleep?

We sleep simply because we need rest. As we sleep, the functioning of our body shifts into another gear. Thus, as we sleep, many phenomena, such as growth, healing and muscle-building occur. When we wake up, we feel refreshed and energised, because our system has recharged itself as it was not expending energy in any kind of activity. In fact, sleeping also helps improve our memory and even our mood!

21. Why do we dream?

Our brains are huge stores of memories and information. Thus, even when we do not remember certain things, facts or people, they are still safely stored inside our brain. Some scientists believe that, when we sleep, the brain subconsciously creates a mix of the things from its store, our emotions and moods. Hence, a dream is created. This is why dreams are often bizarre, they say.

22. What is sleepwalking?

Sleepwalking is a disorder in which a person walks in his or her sleep. Typically, the person's eyes will be shut, but whatever they are doing, they will do as if they are awake and can see. It usually happens at night and the next day, the person will not remember any of it when they awake. The most common cause for sleepwalking is high degree of stress, lack of sleep and drinking or taking medicines. The brain remains active even after the person has slept and makes the person continue to do things in his/her sleep. It is also genetically determined, so that it can be passed from generation to generation. The first few hours of sleep called the 'slow wave' or 'deep sleep' stage is when a person may sleepwalk. It can be overcome by relaxing before one goes to sleep, by listening to music or reading, keeping a regular schedule and sleeping in peaceful surroundings with no noise and lights.

23. Is time the same everywhere?

As the Earth rotates around the Sun, one part of Earth has day whereas the opposite part has night. In the olden days, this created problems for people who travelled from one country to another. The varying train time-tables left them confused. This problem of varying time was solved by creating a standard process of time zones. In this system, the world is divided into 24 time zones and every country has its own time zone with respect to Greenwich, England as zero degrees longitude. This is known as the Greenwich Mean Time or GMT.

24. What is a calendar?

A calendar is a system of organising units of time over an extended period for social, religious and business purposes. The units of time are based on the rotation of Earth on its axis (the day), the revolution of Earth around the Sun (the year) and the revolution of Moon around Earth (the month).

25. What is a Leap Year?

We know that the Earth goes through both rotations and revolutions: rotation means that the Earth rotates about a tilted axis, because of which we experience day and night, with each rotation lasting 24 hours. Revolution means that the Earth revolves around the sun, on its orbit. While we know a revolution to take 365 days to complete, actually, it takes 365 days and 6 hours. Thus, after four years, these extra hours add up to 24 hours, which is the equivalent of a day. Therefore, every four years, we add an extra day to the month of February, so that our calculation of the Earth's revolution stays right. Thus, every four years, we observe a Leap Year, with 366 days.

26. What makes the weather change?

The Earth spins on a slightly tilted axis. Also, when the Earth goes around the Sun, its distance from the Sun changes over the period of the year. Therefore, sunlight strikes the Earth at different angles at different times of the year. This causes uneven heating of the atmosphere and creates areas of high and low pressure. Wind blows from areas of high pressure to areas of low pressure. This movement leads to changes in weather phenomena, such as, humid Monsoons, dry Summer winds or cold Winter storms.

27. What is the ozone layer?

Ozone is a compound formed by three atoms of oxygen. The ozone layer is a layer in the upper portion of the Earth's atmosphere, which contains a heavy concentration of ozone. This layer prevents direct sunlight from hitting us on the Earth by absorbing a large portion of its ultraviolet radiation. Thus, the ozone layer is good for us, as it saves us from harmful radiation from the Sun. However, due to increasing pollution, the ozone layer is thinning down. Thus, we should prevent pollution in order to save ourselves.

28. Why is sunlight dangerous?

Sunlight is not always dangerous, but under certain conditions it can be harmful to human beings. The Sun's rays do not merely contain heat and light but also various kinds of electromagnetic radiation. Its ultraviolet radiation cannot penetrate deep into our bodies, but it does harm our skin and eyes. In fact, excessive Sun exposure is also said to cause skin cancer, apart from stingy sunburns. Therefore, we should protect ourselves from excessive Sun exposure by using hats, sunglasses and sunblock.

29. What is lightning?

Lightning is a bright flash of light that occurs during a thunderstorm. During a thunderstorm, the air rises and falls with great speed. This leads to the separation of positive and negative electric charges in the air. Thus, electricity builds up between these positively and negatively charged particles of the air. This electricity is released from the air in the form of lightning bolts. An average lightning bolt can light up a regular bulb for two to three months! Also, the air around a bolt is hotter even than the Sun!

30. Why do we see lightning before we hear thunder?

We see lightning before we hear thunder because light travels much faster than sound. Also, lightning is actually the cause of the thundering sound. As a bolt of lightning travels from a cloud towards the ground with immense speed, it cuts a pathway through the air. This pathway is called a Channel. After the lightning bolt has passed through the Channel, the vacuum fills up with air again. It is the sound of the air collapsing back into the empty space, which we hear as thunder.

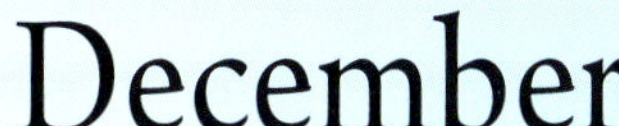

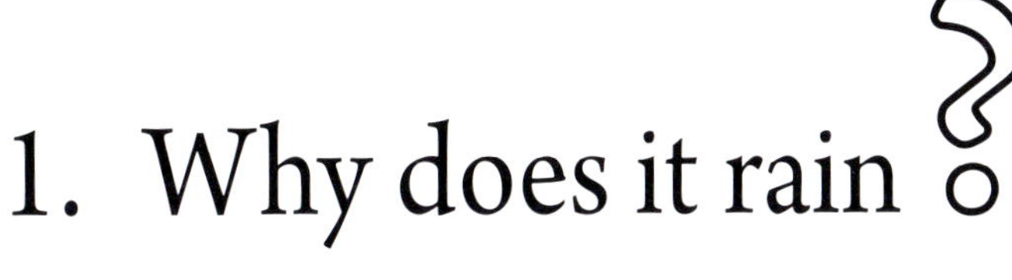

1. Why does it rain?

The air in our atmosphere has the capacity to hold water in it, in the form of vapour. The level of water vapour in the air increases through evaporation. This content of vapour in our air is measured by the air's humidity. If there is more vapour in the air, it is more humid. Similarly, clouds consist of water in the form of small droplets. When the air and clouds become too heavy to contain any more water vapour, they return the water to the Earth in the form of droplets. This causes rainfall.

2. What is fog?

Fog is actually a form of cloud but lies much closer to the ground level. Like clouds, fog consists of tiny droplets of water suspended in the air. Normally, through evaporation, water vapour rises high up in the air. Only when it reaches a high altitude does the vapour cool enough to condense into tiny water drops or clouds. However, sometimes, during cool nights the vapour condenses nearer to the surface of the Earth, forming fog. Greater the saturation of the air, denser is the fog. Sometimes, when the saturation is even larger, it results in drizzling, much like that by an actual cloud.

3. When do rainbows form?

Rainbows form when there is rainfall and sunshine in the sky at the same time! Sunrays look white to us but they are actually made up of seven different colours. Rainbows form in this strange condition because sunlight can pass through the water droplets from the rainfall. Thus, when sunrays pass through transparent water droplets, the droplets break up or refract the white ray into the seven colours that formed it. Hence, we see a rainbow where there is sunshine during or immediately after rainfall!

4. Why is the sky blue?

The air around us contains millions of extremely small particles called molecules. These molecules are not visible to the naked eye. When sunlight passes through these molecules, they scatter its white light into the seven colours it is actually made up of. Of those seven, red, orange and yellow colours pass straight through the molecules. Blue colour, however, is unable to pass through and is reflected by the molecules. Thus, when millions of molecules scatter blue light, the entire sky looks blue to us!

5. Why is the sunset orange?

At sunset, the molecules in the air do not have direct sunlight passing through them. Thus, the molecules are able to scatter much less of the blue colours now. In fact, most of the blue light is scattered away from our line of sight during sunset. Only red and orange light can be seen by our eyes then, because they have longer wavelengths. Hence, a sunset looks orange, red or even pink.

6. What are the different seasons?

There are many seasons that people experience around the world. Seasons are differentiated by a change in weather that then remains constant for a certain period of time, usually measurable in months. Summer is the season when the weather is warm. Winter is the cold season. Spring and Autumn are opposite seasons, because flowers bloom and the grass turns green during Spring, but there are no flowers and the trees shed their leaves during Autumn. Also, there is the Monsoon season, during which we enjoy a lot of rainfall. Interestingly, the areas to the north and south of the equator experience opposite seasons. Thus, when it is Summer in the northern hemisphere, it is Winter in the southern hemisphere!

7. What are Monsoons?

The word Monsoon comes from the Arabic word Mausam, which literally means season, or seasonal wind. Monsoons are seasons that mark the reversal of the wind flow. When the winds reverse their direction, they always lead to some kind of precipitation, like rainfall. There are a number of monsoon systems in the world, the most important of them being the West African and Asia-Australian monsoons.

8. What is hail?

Hail is a form of precipitation, much like rainfall or snowfall. When clouds become thunderstorm clouds and the upperlayers of the atmosphere are severely cold, small stones of ice fall from them. The precipitation of these pieces and lumps of ice is known as hail. Hail stones can be anything from 5 to 500 millimetres in diameter.

9. What is a blizzard?

A blizzard is a situation that arises during severe winter. During a blizzard, the temperature is extremely low, the weather is stormy with strong winds and thick or heavy snowfall. When blizzards are even graver than usual, the temperature can fall below 10 degrees Fahrenheit, winds blow faster than 45 metres per hour and it is almost impossible to see around, even in the immediate vicinity.

10. What is a sandstorm?

As the name suggests, a sandstorm is a phenomenon, wherein dry wind blows with great strength and speed. Since sandstorms occur in desert areas, they create and carry with them large clouds of dust and sand. The environment around a sandstorm is extremely dusty and thick with sand flying in all directions. In such a situation, it is impossible to see properly, or even keep our eyes open.

11. How fast do hurricanes spin?

Hurricane is the name given to a storm that occurs in tropical areas of the world. Hurricanes spin at various speeds. Based on their strength, they are ranked on a scale of 1 to 5. Hurricane Katrina, that occurred in the New Orleans in 2005 was extremely severe and was a category 5 hurricane. On an average, a hurricane spins at 74-155 miles per hour. An interesting fact about these storms is that the winds always spin in the counter-clockwise direction.

12. What is a twister?

A twister, also known as a tornado or cyclone, is a kind of storm. It is characterised by serious thunderstorms, extremely thick rainfall and hail, along with lightning. Winds blow with great speed and change direction very quickly, seeming to twist from one direction to another. This forms a dangerous column of rotating air in a funnel shape. When a twister occurs, the temperature drops very quickly. Also, the thick clouds make everything appear dark. Twisters have been observed on every continent except Antarctica.

13. What causes a tsunami?

Any kind of major disturbance that occurs underwater may cause a tsunami: an earthquake, an explosion or even a volcanic eruption under the sea or ocean can give rise to a tsunami. From its epicentre or point of origin, a tsunami eventually takes the form of a prolonged tidal wave. It can rise up to thirty feet in height, in periods spanning from a few minutes to even a few hours! The great tsunami that occurred in the Indian Ocean in the year 2004 was among the deadliest tsunamis in world history. It was caused because of an earthquake.

14. What is a cloudburst?

A cloudburst is a sudden downpour of rain but is much more severe than simple, regular rainfall. When a cloud bursts, rain pours down thick and fast, much like a shower. A cloudburst can result in almost 100 millimetres of rain in just one hour. In fact, cloudbursts usually last for only a few minutes but they can cause situations much like those of floods.

15. Which train was the first to carry passengers?

The very first passenger train ran from Swansea to Mumbles in South Wales on March 25th 1807. Known as the Mumbles Train, it was pulled by horses and ran along iron tracks. The carriage accommodated 16 people and ran twice a day. The service was first called the Oystermouth Railway.

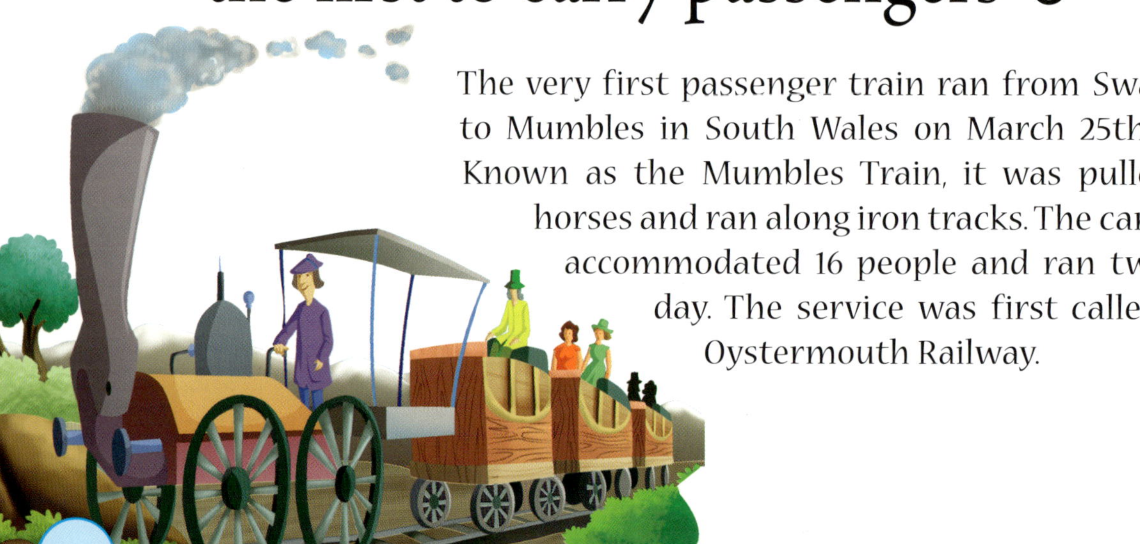

16. What is a locomotive?

A locomotive is a vehicle attached to the train carriage for the purpose of pulling it forward. The locomotive as the name suggests provides motive power to the train. These pull the train in one direction and push it in the other. In modern times, there are self-propelled vehicles running on electric or fuel power that pull the trains.

17. What is a cable train?

Cable trains are especially designed to run on tracks with a steep incline. Since it is difficult for a conventional train to climb the incline, the train, especially freight trains, are pulled by cable lines attached at the top and bottom. Cable trains prove very useful for transporting goods in mines and quarries.

18. What is a bullet train?

A bullet train is a high speed passenger train, which can touch a speed of around 322 kilometres per hour. Originated in Japan, the bullet train or *Shinkansen* is lightening fast because of its sleek aerodynamic body shape and technology that maximises its speed.

19. Which is the longest railroad?

The Trans-Siberian Railroad that connects Moscow with the Russian Far East and Sea of Japan is the world's longest railroad. This rail network covers around 10,000 kilometres, which is equivalent to covering one-third of the Earth's circumference.

20. Can cars run on steam?

The development of the steam engine helped speed up transport greatly. But it took a lot of experimentation until a steam engine was designed that was small and efficient enough to run a car. The earliest steam-powered car was built by Ferdinand Verbiest in 1672. Next came the 'steam wagon' built by Nicholas-Joseph Cugnot in 1769 that hauled cannons for the French Army. In 1801, Richard Trevithick made a steam car that had an internal heat boiler and a vertical cylinder, with a piston moving the wheels. It weighed about 1520 kilograms when fully loaded and attained a speed of 9 miles per hour on a flat road. In England in the 1830s, a regular intercity steam powered bus service was started but the heavy taxes did not allow them to survive.

Steam cars could take some time to warm up, but once they were ready, they could be driven off at once. In 1923, Abner Doble developed an automatic boiler and burner that allowed the car to be started with the turn of a key. The first usable steam car was built in 1899 in Connecticut. The best selling steam car was the 'Stanley Steamer', produced from 1896-1924. The World Land Speed record was broken by a steam powered 'Stanley', driven by Fred Marriot in 1906. This car achieved 127 miles per hour at Ormond Beach, Florida.

21. What fuels do cars use?

The most commonly used fuel is petrol or gasoline, a fossil fuel. Diesel is also made from petroleum and is also used as a cheaper option to petrol. However, there are alternative bio-fuels that are produced from organic waste, like animal and vegetable fats, and other natural waste products. Alcohol fuels, such as ethanol methanol, butanol and proponal are also used, but vehicle engines have to be specially designed to run on these fuels. These alcohols can also be mixed with petrol and diesel. The racing car circuit, the Indy, used methanol for 40 years, before switching to ethanol. This is far more efficient than petrol and diesel. Electricity is also used to power cars and often hybrid versions with electricity and petrol engines are made. A serious effort is being made to make hydrogen-powered vehicles. In these cars, hydrogen fuel cells take in hydrogen and water and convert it into electricity. In the future, it seems likely that cars will be powered by electricity, bio-fuels and hydrogen cells, once the fossil fuels are exhausted.

22. What is an Electric Car?

An electric car is an automobile which is runs on an electric motor. It makes use of batteries that are charged by electricity, hence making use of electric energy and not energy produced by fuel combustion. Electric cars are more beneficial in many ways as compared to conventional cars that use petrol or diesel to run. A significant benefit is the reduction of urban air pollution, as they do not emit harmful exhaust pollutants. There are also reduced greenhouse gas emissions. Use of electric cars decreases consumption of fossil fuels and helps to conserve various resources.

23. Who were the first people to fly across the Atlantic Ocean?

Charles A. Lindbergh, an American pilot was the first person who flew non-stop across the Atlantic Ocean. On May 20, 1927, he took off in his airplane, 'The Spirit of St. Louis' from Roosevelt Field near New York City. Flying northeast along the coast, he flew over Nova Scotia and Newfoundland. He headed out over the Atlantic, aided by a magnetic compass and airspeed indicator towards Ireland. When he landed in less than 34 hours after his departure from New York, Lindbergh became the first person to fly solo across the Atlantic Ocean.

Amelia Earhart was the first woman to fly across the Atlantic in 1932. She received many honours throughout her life. She was a writer as well and founded 'The Ninety Nines', an organisation for female pilots. She disappeared during a solo flight across the globe over the central Pacific Ocean in 1937, and was declared dead.

24. How high can airplanes fly?

The Karaman Line at an altitude of 328,000 feet/62.1 miles high, is considered by many to be the edge of space. Most airplanes, however, fly much below this altitude, at about 20,000-40,000 feet. Even though most aircraft can fly till an altitude of 50,000 feet or more, it is not commercially viable.

25. Which is the fastest airliner?

Commercial airliners travel slower than the speed of sound and usually cruise between 500 and 600 miles per hour (mph). The fastest planes can travel at greater than Mach III, or three times the speed of sound which is about 770 mph. Thus, the Vickers (BAe) VC-10, which flies at Mach 0.855 (650 mph), the Boeing 747-8 launched in late 2009, and the Boeing 777 are the fastest airliners in the world.

26. How far can airlines travel?

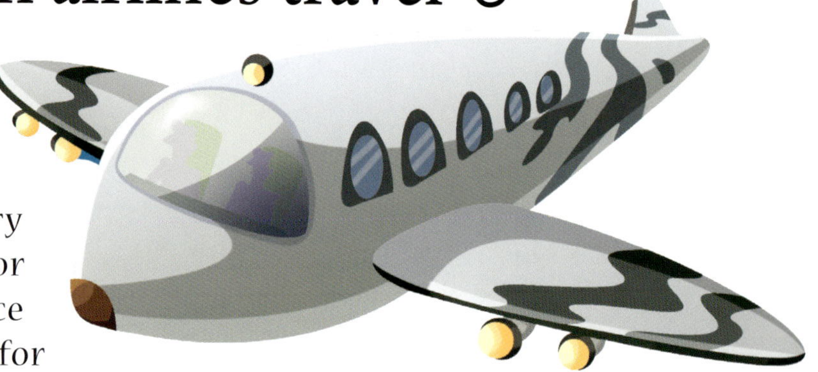

The distance that an airline can travel depends on how big the plane is, how much fuel it can carry and how fast it can fly. For example, a long distance Boeing 747-400ER can fly for 8,826 miles, with fuel left over in reserve. Because they can carry a large amount of fuel, they can fly across the ocean without stopping. Smaller airplanes can travel several hundred miles before they need to refuel. Therefore, by calculating how much fuel is used per hour of flight, a pilot can calculate how far the plane can fly.

27. Who were the first to fly across the Pacific Ocean?

Charles Kingsford-Smith and Charles T. P. Ulm landed in Brisbane, Australia, having become the first pilots to fly across the Pacific. As the first person who flew across the Pacific in 1928, Charles Kingsford-Smith contributed greatly to aviation. Like Lindbergh who crossed the Atlantic, he too is known as one of the most important figures of the Golden Age of Aviation.

28. What is a network?

A network is a series of points that connect routes of communication. A simple example would be the many telephones poles (points) from which the telephone connections are given and the wire strung along the pole (routes of communication). Networks are capable of being connected with other networks and contain branches or sub-networks. There are different types of networks. A computer network is a group of computers that are connected to each other for the purpose of communication. These are usually connected to each other through a master computer or server. A computer network allows resources and information to be shared. In LANs or local-area networks, the computers are geographically close together, such as within the same building. On the other hand, in WANs or wide-area networks, the computers are farther apart and are connected by telephone lines or radio waves.

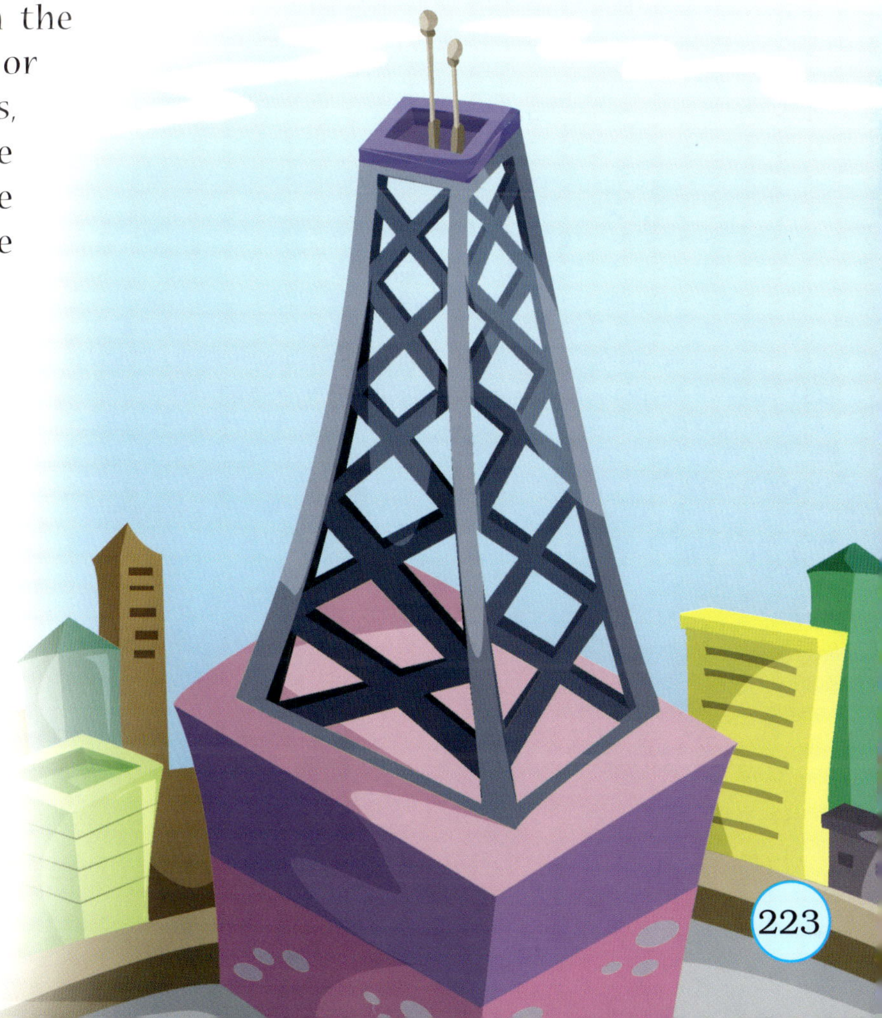

29. What is 'www'?

The initials 'www' stand for World Wide Web. This is a system of interlinked text documents (hypertext) that are contained on the Internet. It is the first part of the site address that you type when you look for a site. The World Wide Web has information of all kinds—with a web browser, you can see web pages that may contain text, images, videos and other multimedia. When you click on a certain part of the page to reach some other image/information, what you are doing is activating the hyperlink that takes you there. Technically, the World Wide Web is defined as 'all the resources and users on the Internet that are using the Hypertext Transfer Protocol (HTTP)', which is a well-defined set of parameters that makes the Internet work.

30. What is a website?

A website is a collection of web pages or Internet files that are part of a single location/site. It could be made by an individual/company and be only about a specific topic. These pages are held together by hyperlinks. The first page is usually called the 'home' page, and is accessed when you type the domain name or Internet Protocol (IP) address into the browser. The browser search engine will look through the network and take you straight to a list of related sites. Each site is hosted by a web server (through the Internet, through a private local area network/party)—this is usually paid for by the person/company who puts up the site.

31. What is a wireless network?

A wireless network refers to any type of computer or telecommunications network that transmit signals without using wires. In these systems, a remote information transmission system uses electromagnetic waves, such as radio waves. Transmission towers at appropriate locations keep the required signal strength. Wireless receivers or antennae catch these signals. The WAN or Wide Area Network and the LAN or Local Area Networks are mainly wireless networks now, making it easy to communicate and use computers and the Internet.

TITLES IN THIS SERIES

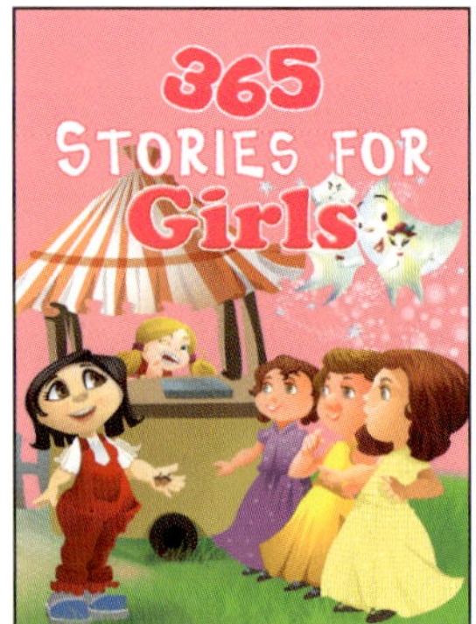

ISBN: 978-93-80070-84-1

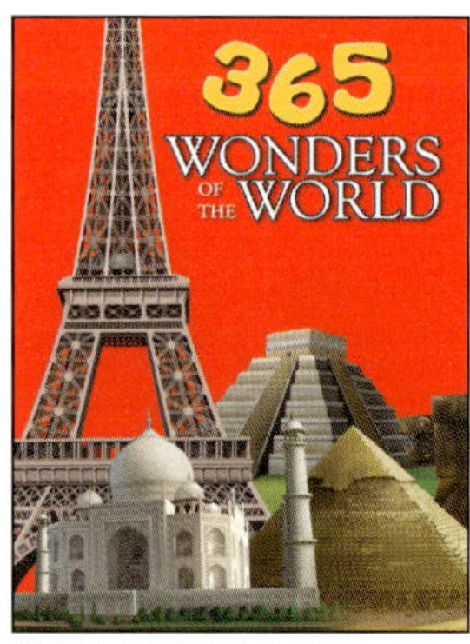

ISBN: 978-93-80069-35-7

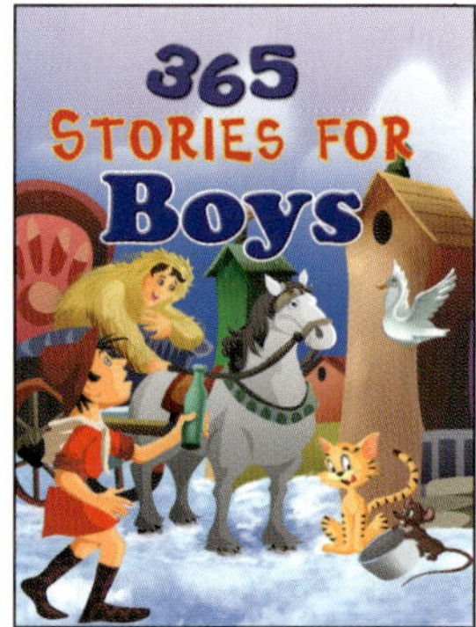

ISBN: 978-93-80070-83-4

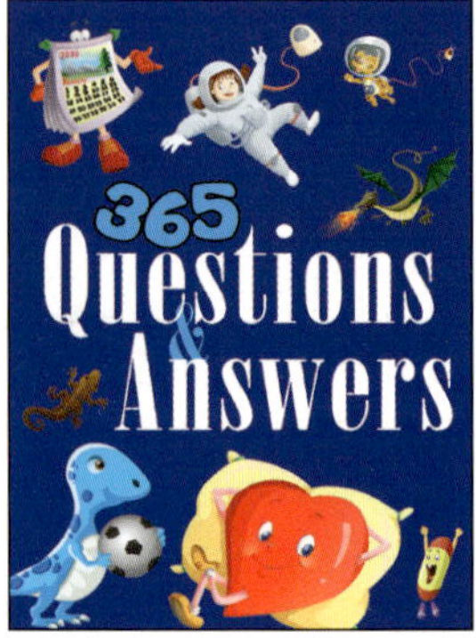

ISBN: 978-93-80070-79-7

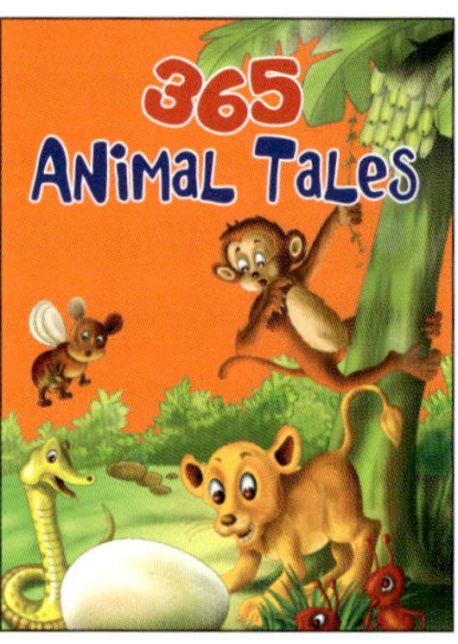

ISBN: 978-81-87107-52-1

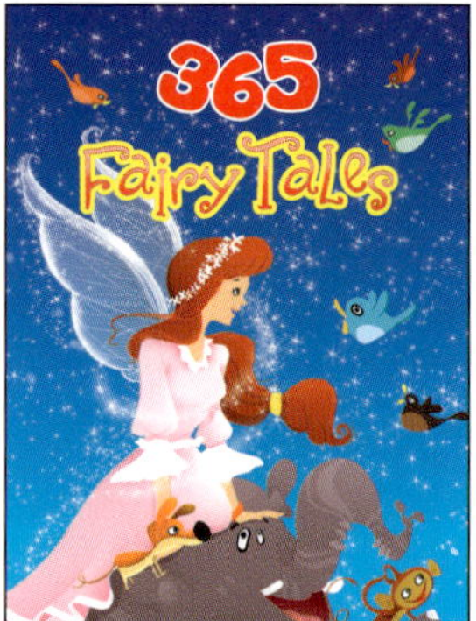

ISBN: 978-81-87107-55-2

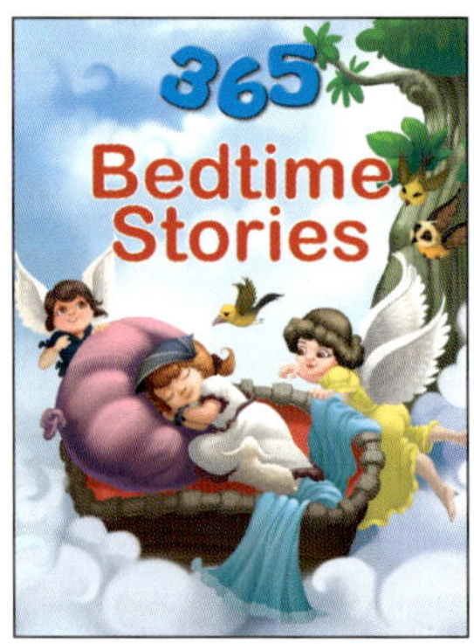

ISBN: 978-81-87107-53-8

ISBN: 978-93-81607-57-2

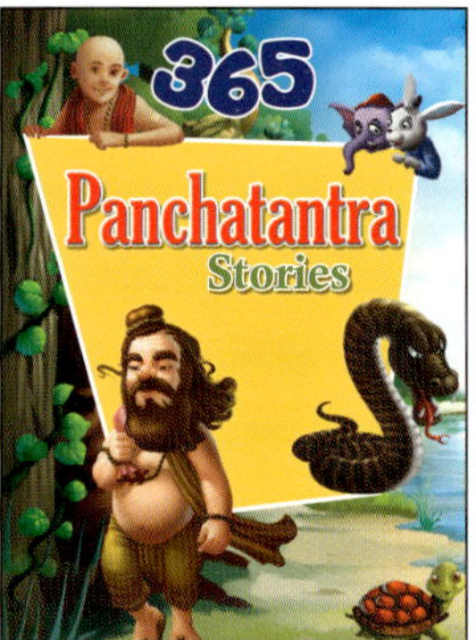

ISBN: 978-81-87107-58-3

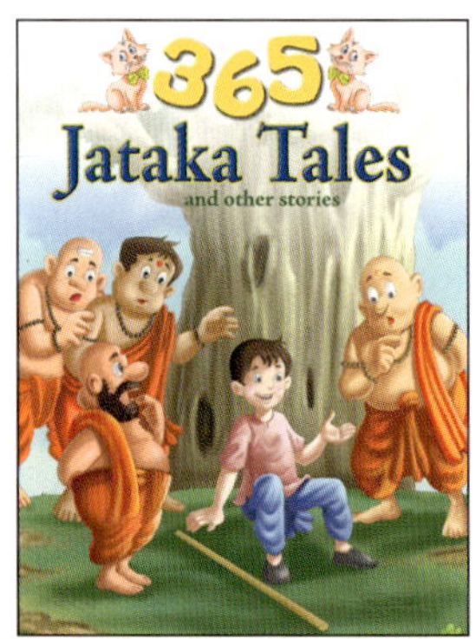

ISBN: 978-81-87107-57-6

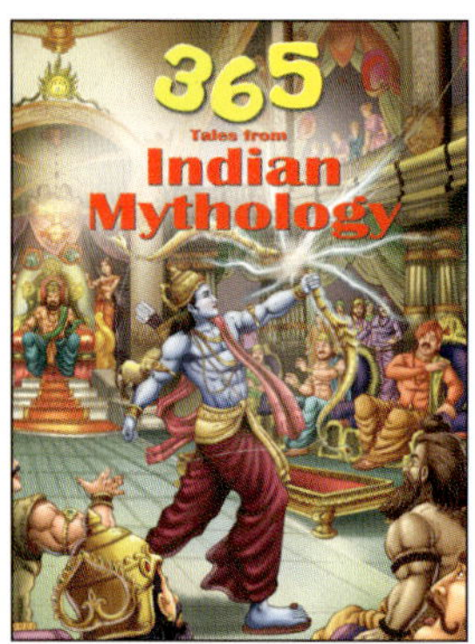

ISBN: 978-81-87107-46-0

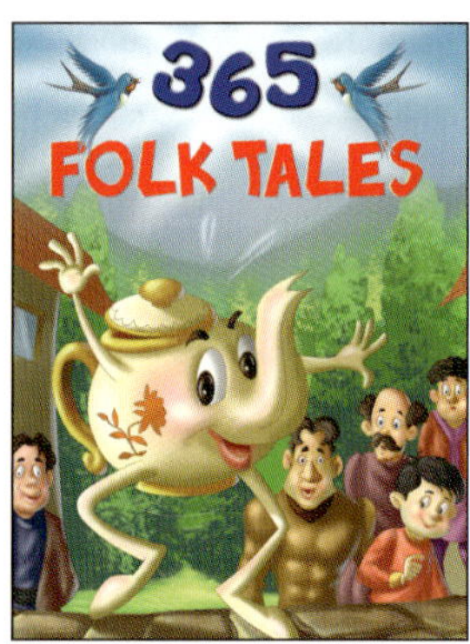

ISBN: 978-81-87107-56-9